Skate Your Personal Best

The Skaters Companion

Sandra Foster, Ph.D.
Tracy Prussack

Rudi Publishing

San Francisco

Rudi Publishing

12 Geary Street, Suite 508

San Francisco CA 94108

1-800-999-6901

rudi3@ix.netcom.com

PRINTED IN THE UNITED STATES

Vaughan Printing, Nashville TN

Other titles in the *Skate Your Personal Best* series include:

> *Skate Your Personal Best: A Guide for Mastering Intermediate and Advanced Technique, Achieving Optimal Performance Skills, and Skating Excellence*
> ISBN 0-945213-27-1 $29.95 paper

> *Skate Your Personal Best: Sound Advice*
> ISBN 0-945213-29-8 $19.95 audio tape

If you have suggestions for additional, helpful items to include in future editions of *The Skaters Companion*, please send them to "Skate Your Personal Best Feedback" c/o Rudi Publishing.

Contents

Welcome to Our Team!

Welcome to *Skate Your Personal Best—The Skater's Companion*. This is the yearly journal that we have created so you can plan each skating year, whether you skate competitively or recreationally. This journal is designed to take you through every step that will help you reach your goals for skating your personal best this year. *The Skater's Companion* corresponds to our manual, *Skate Your Personal Best*, chapter by chapter. In the following pages, you will find an interactive method for learning the latest sport psychology skills that can help you get the most out of your lessons and practice so you can master new elements faster and with less frustration. We have created questions for you to answer and exercises that personalize the process of learning to skate well as you keep your life balanced with other things that may be important to you— family, friends, school, your job, and interests outside of skating.

Figure skating is an exciting and demanding athletic activity that also has a strong artistic component. While skaters who achieve great success are those who skate because they love the sport and skate for their own personal reasons, they know they cannot do it alone. Olympic skaters and National and World Champions all have teams— a coach, sometimes assistant coaches, choreographers, off-ice instructors who help with conditioning, sometimes a sport psychologist, and of course, supportive family members.

Our team is like that, too. Tracy Prussack is an experienced coach recognized by other professionals and her students for her excellence in teaching. She also skated her own personal best, even qualifying for the Olympic Trials with her brother in pairs. They were U.S. National Junior Pair champions and the first pair team to land a side-by-side triple Salchow in a U.S. National competition. Tracy turned pro after recovering from a serious injury and went on to perform with such companies as Disney on Ice.

My formal title is Sandra Foster, Ph.D., but I have also come be known as "Sam." I am a counseling and sport psychologist who coaches clients in the mental skills that bring out their personal best in business, performing arts, and athletics. I studied classical ballet for years, and I also learned some of the very basic moves of skating as a young girl.

Tracy and I teamed up to bring figure skaters the combination of performance enhancement psychology and outstanding technical training. This workbook shows you how we teach skaters to reach their skating excellence goals while valuing their development as people.

Tracy has gathered a team of great professionals. Kevin Peeks is a former national and international competitive skater who also skated professionally in many shows and tours. He has been coaching for eight years and works closely with Tracy. Louis Vachon is a coach and an experienced choreographer who designs unique programs for singles and pairs skaters. John Brancato is a choreographer and coach with a background in professional skating.

Donna Burden is a registered athletic trainer and a physical therapist who grew up in a skating family and was herself a competitive skater. She is the USFSA Team physical therapist and accompanied the United States' competitors to Nagano. Her contribution is her wealth of knowledge about skating-specific conditioning and injury prevention. Chris Conte is a colleague of Tracy's who does outstanding choreography. Julie DiGiallorenzo provides Tracy's students and other skaters with off-ice conditioning programs for strength and flexibility.

Tracy also knows that parents and other family members are the heart of a skater's support system. She spends a lot of time communicating with parents, keeping them informed, responding to questions, and involving them closely in all the planning for the year. That's our team. Who is on your team? Write their names in the space below.

These are the people on my skating team: Elaine, Lindia, Neil, Sarah, Valeri, Mom + Dad, Vicki

What Personal Best Skating Really Means and How It Can Help You

Tracy and I draw our inspiration from a philosophy of "personal best." We describe this philosophy as pursuing a goal and putting effort toward something that is important for your own reasons, not just to please someone else or to gain another person's approval. We work hard at our coaching because we feel a strong desire from the inside to do so. We both love what we do, and our commitment to our work is strong.

When we work with skaters, we encourage each person to discover his or her own reasons for skating. Our experience tells us that young people and adults who skate because they love the sport seem to enjoy their learning more. When a skater loves skating and desires to skate as well as he or she can, we see a more joyful process of learning the technical skills and becoming more artistically aware on the ice.

Personal best skating also means that your main comparison is to compare yourself to your own progress. Comparisons with other skaters may be useful at certain times, such as when it makes sense to do an objective, factual evaluation of similarities and differences. Your coach would be making this kind of objective comparison—along with consulting the USFSA Rule Book to see what's required—when deciding what elements should be in your short program. Another example would be the consideration of what elements and artistry had gone into last year's winning program at regional competitions at your level. You and your coach could then objectively compare this to what you can do in your own program for the coming season.

To Tracy and me, personal best skating means that a skater cares about the *process* of developing the physical skills of skating—a process that takes many years because skating is such a demanding and complicated sport. A personal best skater enjoys this process of "growing" his potential as much or even more than he cares about the outcomes—winning medals, making money, or becoming famous. Personal best skating means focusing on performance goals like "I will perform my very best during this test, exhibition, or competition" rather than being preoccupied by an outcome goal, such as becoming rich from skating.

Skaters who constantly think about the future and winning may find it hard to be happy with their small improvements from regular practice. They may find themselves feeling nervous at competitions and worrying about losing or looking foolish. Some may even quit skating. Before they leave the sport, they can spend much of their time on the ice being unhappy and frustrated.

Tracy, a seasoned coach, knows that excellent skating takes many years to develop. This process can be satisfying if a skater allows himself to appreciate finally landing a new jump and has been patient with himself through many falls while learning the element. If he skates for the fun of it, he'll probably get out of bed more easily each morning to go to a cold rink to practice.

Now we encourage you to think about *you and your skating*. Answering the next few questions will help you see what gets *you* out of bed in the morning to skate.

What are my personal reasons for skating? *B/C I like it + think It's fun to land hard jumps.*

Looking at my reason(s) above, does it seem that I skate for myself? ☑ **Yes** ☐ **No**

Who are the people in my life who want me to skate? *Me, My parents*

Do I want to skate for myself more than he/she/they want me to skate? ☑ **Yes** ☐ **No**

Personal Best Goal-Setting

An important part of doing something well is setting goals. A goal is an objective you want to achieve, or an aim toward which you will direct your hard work and energy. In our view, personal best skating means setting goals, but setting them in a way that may be different from some other things you've read.

First, since personal best skating emphasizes you and your progress, it is helpful in setting goals to talk with your coach, usually with your parents present. If you are an adult skater, another person who cares about you and your skating may want to have input as you set your goals.

Ask your coach to give you his or her observations about your potential. Ask for your coach's opinion about how far you might go in your skating. Things to consider are your age, how much time you have each week to train, whether you seem to have the physical coordination and balance to land double and triple jumps, and how much you enjoy the artistic aspect of skating.

After talking with your coach, write down what your strengths are and what

skating level your coach thinks you could reach. _____

_____

_____

_____

Write down any specific goal(s) your coach suggested. _____

_____

_____

Write down anything else your coach suggested that you should work on during the

coming year. My jumps + skating smoothly

Personal best goal-setting gives your parents an important role. We encourage you to talk with them before deciding what your goals are. Here are some questions that Tracy wants her skaters and their parents to answer before defining goals for the coming season.

My parents have the financial resources for me to skate 18 (or more is have-time) *practice sessions*

per week.

My parents have the financial resources for me to have 15 *lessons per week*

with my coach or assistant coach. These lessons will be 30 *minutes long.*

Transportation for these lessons and practice sessions will be provided by

Mom

My parents have said that I can enter the following competitions that are local and

within driving distance: Princton lake place, NJ concile, Hershey

This year, the main qualifying competition will be held in NJ (Pensackin)

(name of town or city). My parents are planning for me to go. ☒ *yes* ☐ *no*

I have talked to my parents about entering the following out-of-town non-qualifying competitions. They have agreed to pay for me to go to the following:

(if none, write"none") Hershey, Lake Placid

_____

_____

When Tracy and I help skaters think about goals that fit with skating your personal best, we remind them that it helps *to focus on things over which they have control*. They have already talked to Tracy about what is possible for them given their own physical potential. They have also talked with their parents (or if adult skaters, with the other important person in their life) about what is affordable in terms of training, entering competitions, and traveling to competitions.

As you think about your goals, ask yourself these questions to see if your goal is a personal best skating goal.

Am I aiming for something that is under my control?
Winning gold medals isn't entirely under your control since skating is a judged sport. However, you and your coach can plan your training around those artistic and technical qualities that judges look for and mark, components clearly specified in the USFSA Rule Book. A goal that specifies your mastering two new advanced spins to include in your long program *is* something that you can take control over in your lessons and practice. An objective like this would be an appropriate personal best goal.

It is helpful to remember that you don't have absolute control over the placements that judges make but that you can be prepared in those areas that judges look for and evaluate. In contrast, you have little control over how your competitors perform, so focusing on your own skating as you train and while at competitions is a good strategy.

Is the objective of this goal something I have control over?_____

_____

Is my goal an objective that is observable (something I can see)?

A goal such as "I want to skate with more confidence" may be desirable for you to pursue. In that form, however, progress toward your goal may be difficult to observe until you define more specifically what confidence will look like to you. If what you mean by "lack of confidence" is that you skate around many times before attempting a jump, you could rewrite your goal this way: "I will skate confidently by attempting each jump the very first time I approach."

How would you define "to skate confidently" in a way that is observable to you (so that you'll know when you reach that goal)? <u>When it doesn't take a lot of thought - comes natural, consistent</u>

Is my goal clearly stated and definite enough so I will know when I reach it? Do I have a target date for achieving it?

You may want to become more accurate in executing the elements you are learning. Stating a goal such as, "I want to improve my technical marks" is desirable but vague. You won't know when you reach this goal.

You might rewrite the goal as: "I want to land my double Lutz correctly in practice seven out of every ten attempts by the date of the main qualifying competition." Now the goal is clear and definite. You have set clear criteria for improvement (landing correctly seven out of every ten attempts), and you have a target date for reaching that goal. Your technical marks in competition could improve if you had fewer deductions for incorrectly landed double Lutz jumps in your programs, so this is a desirable goal as well.

What would be an example of a clear, definite goal for improving your spirals?

<u>I will be able to hold my leg higher by June 16</u>

Am I aiming for something that is realistic given my coach's assessment of my physical capabilities?

If you have been having great difficulty getting your single jumps mastered, it's unrealistic to set a goal of landing a triple Axel this year. A more realistic goal would be: "During this six-month time period, I will improve my technique on my single jumps so I can be prepared to learn my double jumps. I will work in the harness and land my double Salchow by the end of this training season" (and specify the date).

Think about a realistic goal that builds on something you are currently learning but haven't quite mastered. <u>I will Land D.Axel by Lake Arrowhead + land D.Lutz more consistently, outside edge by June 16.</u>

Is my goal stated in terms of what I want to do rather than what I want to avoid doing? For example, if your goal is to "stop falling so much on my double Salchow," your mind is getting a message that is mostly about falling. A better way to state your goal is in proactive, positive words such as: "I will land my double Salchow consistently, every eight out of ten attempts, within six months" (and specify the date).

Try rewriting, "I won't pop my toe loop jump anymore." _____

_____

_____

Is my goal something I want to do and am I willing to put the time and effort into it? It may be exciting to state the goal: "I will skate singles at Novice level and consistently land two different, difficult double and triple jump combinations, and also find a pairs partner to compete at Intermediate level." However, finding the time, energy, and financial resources to skate both singles and pairs may be more than you can comfortably handle, if you have school or family obligations or a busy social life you'd rather not cut back on.

Think carefully about a time in the past when you felt you were really excited about a goal that you were working hard to achieve because you really wanted it. Write down what that goal was in the space below. _____

_____

_____

Writing out your goals gives you a chance to evaluate them in light of these questions. You can see if each goal challenges you, but doesn't overwhelm you. You can evaluate whether you are working on something that you have control over. You can see if you have written a goal you can keep track of, measure your progress in, and have a date for reaching it.

We want to say a little more about outcome goals versus performance goals. Skaters who reach great success usually have an outcome goal in mind from the time they begin to realize that they love the sport and have talent. For example, 1988 Olympic gold medalist Brian Boitano writes in his autobiography that he had a lifelong dream of skating at the Winter Olympics. His outcome goal was vying for Olympic gold. It took him sixteen years to reach this objective.

What keeps someone showing up for practice for such a long time? A dream goal that is an outcome goal, like "I will compete at the Olympics in Singles," can help a talented skater feel she or he has something to go for.

However, the performance goals set every year are what keep that skater moving through the process of acquiring the technical and artistic skills needed to compete at the Olympic games.

Short-term performance goals show the skater how to improve steadily, day by day, toward his dream. A goal for every practice session and every lesson truly keeps a skater focused and progressing.

It may seem odd, but a skater would be wise to set her dream goal aside as she skates during a competition. Focusing on an outcome goal like winning takes the skater's mind away from what she can control—skating her personal best during her program—which is a true performance goal.

Here is another performance goal for competition: "I will skate my long program with excitement, really getting into my music and keeping my arms and hands in the positions my ballet teacher taught me." This performance goal could help you stay focused on you and your skating— which are things you have control over. This performance goal puts your attention on now, rather than on the future. If you are concentrating on skating your best, rather than winning (which is in the future and not under your control), you are not worrying about either what the judges are deciding or comparing yourself to your competitors. As a result, you are probably going to be much less nervous while you are competing.

Here is a summary of the benefits of performance goals.

- Performance goals define how you want to do something, like "I want to keep my body positioned well on my double Lutz."

- Performance goals, when stated as short-term goals for each practice session and lesson, help you focus on what you are doing at that moment. When you are focused on working on a specific element, like your camel spin, you can make good use of your practice time and can probably master the element more quickly.

- Performance goals keep you going toward your dream goal by defining what you must do to get there.

- Performance goals for competition keep you focused on skating your personal best right *now*. Performance goals can help you focus on managing your emotions and thoughts at the competition site. Repeating a performance goal such as "I will perform my personal best in the long program showing all the artistry I have been practicing" keeps your mind on yourself and not straying off into comparisons with other skaters' programs, costumes, or music.

Think about your dream goal, that is, your ultimate objective for your skating. Keep in mind that most dream goals are long-term aims, requiring many years of training.

What is my ultimate skating goal—my dream goal? TO win Nationals

_____

_____

_____

_____

_____

To make your dream goal seem more real to you, a visual image of it may help. If you like, draw a picture that represents your dream goal in the space below. Or you can use the space for one picture or a collage of pictures that represent your dream goal.

Goals for This Year—the Upcoming Skating Season

❧ *Goals for Competitive Skaters*

List the competitions you plan to skate and your performance and outcome goals

for each one. NJ conch - Top3 , Hershey-Top3

L. Placid - Top3

_____

_____

_____

List any sport psychology goal that could help you perform your personal best this

year. _____

_____

❧ *Goals for Skaters Who Do Not Compete*

List the tests you wish to pass and exhibitions in which you want to participate.

List as a goal any skating camp or clinic that you wish to attend this year.

_____

_____

_____

_____

_____

_____

List any sport psychology goal you have. _____

_____

STEP 1. THINK ABOUT HOW LAST YEAR WENT FOR YOU.

Ask yourself, "how would I evaluate my rate of improvement and my outcomes (tests passed, competition results) during this past year?"

Here is an example for a skater who does not compete: "I passed my moves in the field for Intermediate. I also made progress with my artistic skills because of my ballet class. I still want to coach eventually."

Here is an example for a competitive skater: "I passed my freestyle test for Novice last summer. I skated well at Regionals and went on to Sectionals, but didn't qualify for Nationals. I got deductions for not doing sufficient revolutions on my spins, and was so tired and out of breath at the end of my long program that I finished behind my music."

Write your review of last year's progress. _____

_____

_____

_____

_____

STEP 2. WITH THIS REVIEW OF LAST YEAR IN MIND, WRITE YOUR GOALS FOR THIS YEAR.

Example for a non-competitive skater: "This year, I will work on three double jumps. I will skate in two exhibitions this summer and one during the fall."

Example for a competitive skater: "I will be better conditioned to skate my new programs at the Regional competition and finish them strongly with plenty of energy. I will improve my spins so that I complete the required number of revolutions and reach a greater speed. I will qualify for Sectionals and Nationals."

List your goals for this skating season. _____

_____

_____

_____

_____

If you like, draw a picture (or paste in a picture) in the space below that represents your goals for this coming year.

On the next page is Tracy's goal sheet for the year. You may copy this to use with your coach. Write in your monthly goals under each heading on the goal sheet.

Tracy's Goal Sheet for the Year

	Technical On-Ice Training	Artistic On-Ice Training	Off-Ice Training	Tests	Competitions
January					
February					
March					
April					
May					
June					
July					
August					
September					
October					
November					
December					

Technical Goals

List the technical elements that you will need to master in order to reach your goals for this year.

Moves in the field NOViCe _____

_____

Connecting steps _____

_____

Spins _____

_____

Jumps D.Axel _____

_____

Other elements (for pair skaters or ice dancers) _____

_____

Now list the artistic qualities that you will need to develop in order to reach your goals for the coming year._____

_____

_____

_____

_____

_____

_____

✑ *Your Technical Goals for the Coming Year*

List your technical goals (in measurable terms) for the coming year.

Example One: "I will land my double Axel 60% of the times I attempt it."

Example Two: "I will correct the position on my flying camel and flying sit spin. During the month of September, before Regionals, I will do two program run-throughs during each practice."

List your technical (long-term) goals for the coming year. _____

_____

_____

_____

_____

_____

✑ *Technical Short Term Goals*

In order to reach your long-term goals for the coming year, what short-term goals can help you get there?

Example One: "Each week I will work in the harness with my coach until I get the right feel for my double Axel. I will review videotape of my progress on my double Axel and use it, along with my coach's corrections, to master this jump."

Example Two: "Each week I will spend ten minutes of my lesson time on the flying camel and flying sit spins. I will attend daily stroking classes each week to build up my stamina."

Write the short-term goals necessary to achieve each of your long-term technical goals.

_____

_____

_____

_____

_____

∽ *Barriers and Solutions to Achieving Technical Goals*

What are the possible barriers, if any, to mastering the technical elements you listed on page 17? What can you do to overcome these barriers so that you can reach your goal?

Technical element you want to master _____

Possible barrier _____

What you can do to overcome this barrier? _____

_____

_____

_____

Technical element you want to master _____

Possible barrier _____

What you can do to overcome this barrier? _____

_____

_____

_____

Technical element you want to master _____

Possible barrier _____

What you can do to overcome this barrier? _____

_____

_____

_____

ARTISTIC GOALS

Now list your artistic goals (in measurable terms) for the coming year.

Example One: "I will work on correct arm positions."

Example Two: "I will listen to my music more often so I know it better. I will skate more rhythmically to the beat of my music for both my programs."

Your artistic (long-term) goals for the coming year: _____

_____

_____

_____

_____

⤳ Short Term Artistic Goals

In order for your to reach your long-term goals for the coming year, what short-term goals can help you get there?

Example One: "Each week for the month of May, my parents will pay my ballet teacher to come to the rink to work with me to make my arm positions more graceful."

Example Two: "Each week during April through June, I will have my ballet teacher spend extra time with me in class tapping out rhythms to music. I will also ask her to give me feedback about her observations of me staying with the beat as we do our ballet performance piece at the end of each class."

Write the short-term goals necessary to achieve each long-term artistic goal.

_____

_____

_____

_____

_____

⌒ *Barriers and Solutions to Achieving Artistic Goals*

What are the possible barriers, if any, to mastering the artistic qualities you listed on page 20 ? What can you do to overcome these barriers so you can reach your goal?

Artistic element you want to master —————————————————

Possible barrier ————————————————————————

What you can do to overcome this barrier? ————————————

————————————————————————————————

————————————————————————————————

————————————————————————————————

Artistic element you want to master —————————————————

Possible barrier ————————————————————————

What you can do to overcome this barrier? ————————————

————————————————————————————————

————————————————————————————————

————————————————————————————————

Artistic element you want to master —————————————————

Possible barrier ————————————————————————

What you can do to overcome this barrier? ————————————

————————————————————————————————

————————————————————————————————

————————————————————————————————

ᙍ *The Smallest Short-Term Goal*

The smallest short-term goal you set could be your goal for each practice session and each lesson. Setting a goal like this will help you use your time well and will help you stay focused. To do this, you could talk with your coach and review your long-term technical and artistic goals.

Example: In practice sessions, you are probably working independently, without your coach's input, so you may want to set a goal that you can pursue on your own and one for which you can evaluate your own progress.

Write in a goal to work on in your next practice session.

_____

_____

Date _____

Write in a goal that you and your coach have decided to work on in your next

lesson. You and your coach can both evaluate whether you achieve this lesson goal

or not.

_____

_____

Date _____

You can use the form on the following page to measure goals for your practice sessions and lessons one week at a time. For example, under technical elements you might write "double Salchow." When you fill in "the week of" use the Monday of each week as your starting date.

Measuring Your Weekly Goals

Technical Element	Week of:	Week of:	Week of:	Week of:	Week of:	Week cf:	Week of:

Rate your artitistic progress.   No progress=0   Little Progress=1   Moderate Progress=2   Good Progress=3   Great Progress=4

Your Goals for Competitions This Year

Name of Competition _____

Date _____

Performance Goals _____

_____

Outcome Goal _____

Name of Competition _____

Date _____

Performance Goals _____

_____

Outcome Goal _____

Name of Competition _____

Date _____

Performance Goals _____

_____

Outcome Goal _____

Name of Competition _____

Date _____

Performance Goals _____

_____

Outcome Goal _____

Name of Competition _____

Date _____

Performance Goals _____

_____

Outcome Goal _____

Name of Competition _____

Date _____

Performance Goals _____

_____

Outcome Goal _____

Name of Competition _____

Date _____

Performance Goals _____

_____

Outcome Goal _____

Name of Competition _____

Date _____

Performance Goals _____

_____

Outcome Goal _____

Thinking That Leads to Skating Excellence

Noticing and Identifying Your Negative Thoughts During Lessons

I have this thought . . .

How do I feel after thinking this negative thought? _____

_____

What happens to my skating after I think this negative thought? _____

_____

_____

I have this thought . . .

How do I feel after thinking this negative thought? _____

_____

What happens to my skating after I think this negative thought? _____

_____

_____

Noticing and Identifying Your Negative Thoughts As the Competition Season Approaches

I have this thought . . .

How do I feel after thinking this negative thought? _____

_____

_____

_____

What happens to my skating after I think this negative thought? _____

_____

_____

I have this thought . . .

How do I feel after thinking this negative thought? _____

_____

_____

_____

What happens to my skating after I think this negative thought? _____

_____

NOTICING AND IDENTIFYING YOUR NEGATIVE THOUGHTS DURING COMPETITIONS

I have this thought . . .

How do I feel after thinking this negative thought? _____

_____

_____

What happens to my skating after I think this negative thought? _____

_____

_____

I have this thought . . .

How do I feel after thinking this negative thought? _____

_____

_____

What happens to my skating after I think this negative thought? _____

_____

_____

_____

Noticing And Identifying Your Negative Thoughts Before and During Test Days

I have this thought . . .

How do I feel after thinking this negative thought? _____

_____

_____

_____

What happens to my skating after I think this negative thought? _____

_____

I have this thought . . .

How do I feel after thinking this negative thought? _____

_____

_____

_____

What happens to my skating after I think this negative thought? _____

_____

NOTE: For advice about changing negative thoughts to more positive ones, see the next section and chapter three in the manual.

THE POWER OF OPTIMISM FOR YOUR SKATING

As a sport psychologist, I have observed how a skater's mental attitude has an impact on the quality of his or her skating, regardless of skill level. Physical skills are a *must* in figure skating, and no amount of wishful thinking, visualizations, or relaxation techniques can substitute for mastering the technical elements of skating.

What is also true is that figure skating is a very demanding sport *mentally*. Thus developing your mental training skills can help you express your full physical potential out on the ice, especially in competitions.

In our book *Skate Your Personal Best* we explain the power of optimistic thinking in great detail. Here in the *Skater's Companion*, I briefly summarize what optimism is and guide you through a series of learning exercises.

Dr. Martin Seligman, a psychologist, did the groundbreaking research that showed that the way a person explains what happens to him, whether good or bad, is a typical or characteristic way that person interprets life's happenings. This "explanatory style," as Seligman termed it, can be either pessimistic or optimistic.

When bad events occur, the pessimistic person often makes a bad thing a *personal* one. The pessimist takes it personally, and blames himself excessively, and what involvement other people or circumstances might have had in causing that bad event is not taken into account. As a result, the pessimist feels bad, not just about the bad thing that happened, but about himself as well. His self-esteem keeps dropping. He probably won't look at what he can change around him to keep the bad event from happening again.

The pessimist also explains a bad event to himself as something that will last a long time and feels down and hopeless. The pessimist may likewise generalize his negative view to other parts of his life, then perceive that everything in his life is bad. This generalizing is like a domino effect, with the pessimist thinking that all of his life is a disaster. How much of life is explained as good or bad Seligman called "scope." Pessi-

---

[1] The material in this section first appeared in an article I wrote for the newsletter *Skater's Edge,* in the summer 1996 .

mists see one instance of negativity extending to pretty much everything. For example, being late to a lesson (one negative thing) leads a person to think that everything is awful—her scope of negativity is now global—and she might as well give up on anything going well for the entire day.

Two skaters could be skating at the same level, have similar physical potential, and both be training with good coaches. However, the pessimistic skater has a very different mental experience of a tough day than an optimistic skater does. For example, let's say both skaters have been on a lesson and have repeatedly tried a complicated spin. Both have toppled over several times, despite their best efforts and their coaches' encouragement.

The pessimistic skater is discouraged and feels very upset. With her pessimistic explanatory style, she explains why she is having trouble learning a complex element this way: "I'll never get this move! It's way too hard for me! I should give up skating because I'm just a terrible skater. And I can't keep a boyfriend, and my schoolwork isn't going well, either!" Because she is so upset, this skater will not be able to use her coach's correction. (The corrections are likely to be ignored anyway, because the skater believes it won't make a difference.) She may consider quitting because her pessimism makes it almost impossible to remain hopeful about improving. Enjoying the process of learning is not a part of this pessimistic skater's experience.

The optimistic skater explains her difficulty with the spin in a much different way. She can take responsibility for the tough time she is going through without blaming herself excessively. She does not label herself as a "terrible skater" but recognizes her role in things not working: "I'm tired and I'm not focused. That is probably why it's not working for me. Oh, well, I have school to look forward to, and seeing my friends later today. I can get some sleep and come back to this tommorow."

These explanations for her poor lesson describe circumstances ("tired; not focused") that won't last forever. They are limited in time, and she can fix them. She also limits the scope of the negativity she experienced on the ice by thinking of other things going well for her, even if skating, at that moment, is not. The optimistic skater listens to her coach's correction and tries it out. If it still doesn't go well, the optimistic skater and her coach decide whether she should move on to practice some other element and come back to the challenging spin at the next lesson.

The optimistic skater can keep her skating in perspective. If skating isn't going well, the difficulty won't last too long. She believes that things will get better and that she can change what she is doing for the better. She can contain, or limit the negativity that happened at the rink to just that—and then go on and enjoy the rest of her day.

You may recognize either pessimism or optimism in your explanations when you are having a tough time on the ice. Please understand that explanatory style—that is, pessimism or optimism—is learned from our experiences growing up. No one is a born pessimist or a born optimist. As children, some people see what happens to them and develop a pessimistic explanation for bad and good events, while others acquire an optimistic view.

So optimism is learned, and the good news is that Seligman found a way to train people of any age, from young children to elders, in the skills of optimistic thinking. His research showed that most anyone who has learned to be pessimistic can learn how to generate more optimistic explanations for events. As a result, these new optimists can be more hopeful and help themselves out of discouragement when experiencing setbacks.

We teach you more about optimism in our *Skate Your Personal Best,* and here in the *Skater's Companion* are many examples drawn from skating. Becoming more optimistic will help you in your skating and in other areas of life as well.

We invite you to try the exercises on the next six pages. You are asked to take a close look at the negative thoughts you identified on pages 26 to 29. Then see if you can change these negative or pessimistic thoughts to more optimistic ones, using the examples that are given.

There is real benefit for you in developing your optimism. You are likely to come back much stronger after a setback in a lesson or after a disappointing competition.

∽ *Changing Negative Statements to Optimistic Ones*

Pessimism
———————

Bad things last a long time, even forever.
Examples:
"I will never land this Lutz."
"This bad slump will go on and on."
"Yeah, I got it this time but it won't last."
"I don't want to skate anymore."

Look at pages 26 to 29. What were your negative statements that are similar to these?

——————————————————

——————————————————

——————————————————

——————————————————

——————————————————

——————————————————

——————————————————

Optimism
———————

Bad things are temporary.
There will be a tomorrow and another day for me to skate.
Examples:
"Tomorrow will be better."
"I'm having an off day today."
"I finally got that spin. It will work
  tomorrow, too."
"I can keep this good thing going."

Rewrite your negative (pessimistic) statements as optimistic ones.

——————————————————

——————————————————

——————————————————

——————————————————

——————————————————

——————————————————

——————————————————

◦ *Changing Negative Statements to Optimistic Ones*

Pessimism
————

This jump isn't working. Everything is bad.

Examples:

"I'm falling on all my jumps."

"I can't do this spin, or anything else!"

"Yeah, footwork was OK, but the rest
   of my program was terrible."

"I can't skate! I can't do anything!"

*Look at pages 26 to 29. What were
your negative statements that are
similar to these?*

_____

_____

_____

_____

_____

_____

Optimism
————

*Bad things are limited. One thing may not
be clicking with my skating, but a lot of things
are working.)*

Examples:

"Even if skating is tough, other
   things in my life are OK."

The next try will bring me closer
   to landing that Axel."

"Yeah, this session didn't go
   well. I'll do better on the next one."

"I will put this awful lesson behind me
   and get my homework done."

*Rewrite your negative (pessimistic)
statements as optimistic ones.*

_____

_____

_____

_____

_____

_____

~ *Changing Negative Statements to Optimistic Ones*

Pessimism

*Bad things are totally
my fault. I'm just a failure.*

Examples:

"I just can't do it."

"The only reason I won is because
  the others were too jet lagged."

"I just don't have what it takes."

"I'm a lousy skater and not worth
  much as anything else."

**Look at pages 26 to 29. What were
your negative statements that are
similar to these?**

_____

_____

_____

_____

_____

_____

Optimism

*I take responsibility for my role in bad events.
I try to improve and change what I can by
considering the role of outside
circumstances.*

Examples:

"The ice is pretty mushy today. But I skated
my best."

"I can make this correction and get it
right."

"I think my coach is really tired and
not feeling well. I sensed that and didn't
let it affect me."

"I did work hard for that silver medal."

**Rewrite your negative (pessimistic)
statements as optimistic ones.**

_____

_____

_____

_____

_____

_____

More Practice For Learning Optimistic Thinking To
Enhance My Skating

I have this pessimistic
thought . . .

Write a new optimistic thought.

_____

_____

_____

_____

What is the likely effect on your skating?

_____

_____

I have this pessimistic
thought . . .

Write a new optimistic thought.

_____

_____

_____

_____

What is the likely effect on your skating?

_____

_____

I have this pessimistic thought . . .

Write a new optimistic thought.

_____

_____

_____

_____

_____

What is the likely effect on your skating?

_____

_____

I have this pessimistic thought . . .

Write a new optimistic thought.

_____

_____

_____

_____

_____

What is the likely effect on your skating?

_____

_____

Turn back to your long-term technical goals on page 18.

Write down your thoughts right now about reaching these goals.

_____

_____

_____

Look at your thoughts. *Are they optimistic or pessimistic?* _____

What is the probability (the chance) that you will reach these technical goals?

Rate this probability from 0% to 100%. _____

Can you change any pessimistic thought you notice to a more optimistic thought?

Do that here and write the new optimistic thought.

_____

Turn back to page 20 and look at your long-term artistic goals.

Write down your thoughts about reaching these goals.

_____

_____

_____

Look at your thoughts. *Are they optimistic or pessimistic?* _____

What is the probability (the chance) that you will reach these artistic goals?

Rate this probability from 0% to 100%. _____

Can you change any pessimistic thought you notice to a more optimistic thought?

Do that here. Write the new optimistic thought in the space below.

_____

Learning to Focus, Concentrate, and Manage Distractions

Some Definitions:

Focus—Taking notice of just one thing by narrowing your attention to it and managing distractions. A distraction is something that diverts your attention away from what you want to focus on, like skating.

Concentration—Focusing for a significant period of time.

Being able to focus when you are skating is easier if your reasons for skating are personal best reasons, that is, if you are skating for yourself and because you enjoy the sport.

Review

What are your reasons for skating? _____

_____

Are you skating to please anyone else besides yourself? ☐ *Yes* ☐ *No*

If you checked "yes," who is it that you are trying to please? _____

What might you hope to gain by pleasing this person by skating? _____

_____

Look over your technical and artistic goals again. Are your goals clear?

Check if:

☐   They are specific.

☐   You have a date for reaching that goal.

☐   You have defined the barriers that could interfere with reaching your goals.

☐   You have come up with possible solutions for each barrier.

There are two kinds of distractions:

Internal—things inside your head like thoughts and images, and the way your body feels.

External—things outside yourself that can divert your attention away from skating.

Identifying and Managing Internal Distractions

Check those internal distractions that are a problem for you:

- ☐ Pessimistic thoughts (refer back to pages 26 to 29)
- ☐ You are sleep deprived
- Anxiety about performing well:
  - ☐ Before Test Days
  - ☐ Before Competitions
- ☐ Negative emotions (anger, fear, feeling overwhelmed)
- ☐ Worried you'll get psyched out by your competitors
- ☐ Comparing yourself with other skaters so that you are not thinking about your skating
- ☐ Your health is not OK
- ☐ Current skating injury
- ☐ Worry about reinjury
- ☐ Fatigue

☙ *Being Sleep Deprived*

Tracy and I know that getting enough sleep can be challenging for skaters with busy lives and a demanding practice and lesson schedule. The research on sleep suggests that going to bed at the same time every night and waking up at the same time every morning helps a person feel more rested. Athletes like skaters who are still growing physically may need nine or ten hours of sleep per night. Someone older who has reached his or her maximum height may need eight to nine hours per night. It's hard to get by with less and feel rested enough to focus while on the ice. Fill out the sleep schedule on the next page to see how much sleep you get, on average, during a typical week.

Sleep Schedule		Waking Up Time	Naps (time/length of nap)	Bedtime	Total Hours of Sleep
Current	Monday				
	Tuesday				
	Wednesday				
	Thursday				
	Friday				
	Saturday				
	Sunday				
What you wish was happening	Monday				
	Tuesday				
	Wednesday				
	Thursday				
	Friday				
	Saturday				
	Sunday				

What do you think are the barriers in the way of your getting more sleep?

_____

_____

_____

What are possible solutions to these barriers? _____

_____

_____

_____

_____

WHAT HELPS YOU SLEEP BETTER ONCE YOU GET YOURSELF INTO BED?

☐ A room temperature that is neither too hot or too cold.

☐ Quiet, dark room (*so you don't hear other family members talking or the TV blaring or music playing*).

☐ You haven't just exercised. (*For some people, exercising too late in the evening can cause sleeplessness or 'insomnia.'*)

☐ You have not had coffee or a caffeinated drink right before bed. (*Caffeine makes most people alert and not ready to sleep—soft drinks like Pepsi and Coke contain caffeine. The effects of drinking caffeine can last for hours.*)

☐ You haven't just eaten a heavy or spicy meal. (*You may develop indigestion which can lead to sleeplessness.*)

☐ You haven't just watched a scary or exciting TV show or video. (*The physical arousal*
☐ *from intense TV or movies may make it difficult to fall asleep for several hours.*)

✍ *Techniques For Decreasing Anxiety Before Test Days And Competitions*

BREATHING

Breathing techniques are one of the fastest ways to help you get control of nervousness. Nervousness may be experienced in ways like your heart is pounding, your feet are cold, you feel queasy or shaky. When you slow your breathing down, your heart rate also slows down, helping you to feel calmer and more in control. The following breathing exercises can help when you find yourself worried or nervous or stressed out.

Calming Breath Exercise

This breathing exercise is helpful before a competition or test.

1. Sit down with your back straight and your head leaning against something, if possible. Place your hands, palms down, on your knees. Keep your eyes open.

2. Tighten all the muscles in your body as much as you can, all at once, then let yourself go limp, letting go of the tightness and as much of your nervousness as possible. You will notice a rebound effect, with a feeling of relaxation moving through you.

3. Exhale through your nose as if you are trying to empty the air out of your lungs, and let out a long sigh.

4. Take in a long breath through your nose as you count to yourself from one to five. Feel your diaphragm (abdomen) rise as you do this.
5. Now close your eyes. Exhale completely through your nose as you count to yourself from one to seven.
6. Open your eyes. Start breathing through your nose in a gentle, slow rhythm using this statement to pace yourself: "Breathe in— pause— breathe out."
7. Continue to breathe in this gentle, slow, and rhythmic way for two minutes or more.

Clearing the Tension

This is a good breathing exercise for when you feel particularly stressed out or overwhelmed with too much to do.

1. Sit down with your back straight and your head leaning against something, if possible. Place your hands, palms down, on your knees. Keep your eyes open.
2. Exhale through your nose in one long breath.
3. Inhale a long, deep breath through your nose and hold for a count of three.
4. Exhale through your mouth, as if you are pushing the air completely out of your lungs, making an audible "hah" sound.
5. Inhale another long, deep breath through your nose and hold it for a count of three.
6. Exhale through your mouth again, pushing the air out of your lungs and making the "hah" sound.
7. Repeat steps 5 and 6 once more, then just sit quietly for about two minutes, breathing in a slow, rhythmic manner. Keep your eyes open in a "soft eyes" gaze. (This means you are looking at something straight ahead but without straining your eye muscles or staring.)

Exercise for Quieting an Overloaded Mind Using the Breath

1. Sit down with your back straight and your head leaning against something, if possible. Place your hands, palms down, on your knees. Keep your eyes open.
2. Gently close your eyes and begin to breathe slowly and rhythmically. As you take in each breath, count it to yourself, "one-one," then "one-two," then "one-three," then "one-four," then "one-five." Start your counting over again with "one-one," gently breathing and counting your breaths for about two minutes.

3. If thoughts start to bother you as you do this, just allow them to come and go, without taking notice of any one thought.

4. When you finish, slowly open your eyes. Stretch a bit. Do a few neck rolls, very s-l-o-w-l-y. To do a neck roll, gently and slowly lower your chin toward your chest and hold for three seconds. Then slowly straighten your head and turn it to the right, as if you were trying to touch your right shoulder with your right ear. Straighten your head slowly, and then move your head back, ever so slowly, toward your spine and hold for three seconds. Straighten your head again and then move it slowly to the left, as if you were trying to touch your left shoulder with your left ear, and hold for three seconds. Now straighten your head again and just rest for a few moments.

Quick Progressive Relaxation

This exercise works on the principle of alternately tensing and then relaxing the major muscle groups, in order to feel a "rebound" decrease in tension.

1. Sit down with your back straight and your head leaning against something, if possible. Place your hands, palms down, on your knees. Keep your eyes open.

2. Tense the specific group of muscles (see below) for a count of five.

3. Then let the muscles go limp, allowing them to relax as much as possible.

4. Rest for about ten seconds before tensing the next muscle group.

5. Repeat steps 2, 3, and 4 until you have tensed and relaxed all the muscle groups once.

6. For best results, go through each of these muscle groups in the following order:
    Face—Make a scowling face, clenching your jaw and gritting your teeth.
    Shoulders—Hunch your shoulders up toward your earlobes.
    Abdomen—Tighten the muscles of your abdomen (belly) by sucking in your stomach.
    Arms—Make tight fists with both hands while holding your arms straight out in front of you.
    Legs—Curl your toes back toward your knees while holding your legs straight out in front of you.

7. Now close your eyes and sit quietly for about one minute. You can say calming phrases to yourself, like "My arms and legs are heavy and warm. My mind is quiet. I am feeling more and more relaxed."

Using Imagination Exercises

As a sport psychologist, I have noticed that many people can visualize; that is, they can see internal images as if they were watching a movie in their mind's eye. However, we all have unique ways of experiencing things inside our own minds.

Some people think more in words. Some people experience information that they are thinking about more by feeling it, what we call "kinesthetic" sensing. Each of us is different, so I am giving these exercise instructions for helping you calm yourself by using the word *imagine*.

If you do visualize, that's great. Make your mental images as vivid as you can. If you do not visualize clearly or at all, think about relaxation in your own way, using words or sounds or by feeling the experience of calming down. Here is a set of mental training exercises used by elite and Olympic athletes in many sports. These techniques are done to prepare for competition, to gear up before a difficult practice, or just to rest your mind.

Using Your Imagination to Relax

Sit down with your back straight and your head leaning against something, if possible. Place your hands, palms down, on your knees. Gently close your eyes.

Start to imagine yourself being in a place that you consider relaxing. This place can be real, like a place you have visited while on vacation, or perhaps somewhere outdoors, where you have walked or gone hiking. Examples might be in a mountain cabin, at the beach, at home with a nice fire going in the fireplace on a cold night, or on a lake in a rowboat or sailboat. You can also make up a pleasant place, like a virtual place in a computer game.

Either way, begin to imagine this place. If you visualize, imagine seeing what is around you as vividly as if you were watching a movie. Notice even the small details of where you are. If there is furniture, notice what it is made of and what it looks like. If you are outdoors, see the trees, grass, or flowers as clearly as if you were there. Look up and see the sky above you. Are there clouds? Do you see the sun?

Now imagine hearing the sounds that are part of this place. For example, if you are at the beach, hear the sound of the waves breaking on the shore. Hear the seagulls making their squawking cries. If you are in a forest, imagine hearing the wind blowing gently through the trees. If you are indoors, notice what sounds are present in this place that you are creating in your mind.

Now imagine that you can feel whatever the temperature of the air is. If you are at the beach, imagine feeling the sand under your bare feet. Feel the warmth of the sun on your skin, pleasant but not too hot.

See if you can even imagine the scents associated with the place you are creating. It might be the scent of pine needles if you are in the forest. Imagine the smell of sun and seawater at the beach. If you are inside, imagine the air has a pleasing perfumed scent that you really like and feel calmed by as you are there.

Remain in this place for a few moments, thinking that you can return here at any time you wish, just to relax. In the space below, draw a picture of this special place or paste a photograph or clipping from a magazine that represents this place to you. Give this picture a title.

My special place—where I go to relax in my imagination

Title _____

Draw it here.

More Visualization/Kinesthetic Sensing Exercises for Relaxing

The Pinwheel Relaxation Exercise

1. Sit down with your back straight and your head leaning against something, if possible. Place your hands, palms down, on your knees. Gently close your eyes.
2. Imagine that you can see a pinwheel, the child's toy that turns around on a stick. Or, instead, imagine seeing a windmill. If you do not visualize clearly or at all, imagine that you can feel the motion of a pinwheel or windmill as it turns.
3. See or feel the pinwheel or windmill as stress, spinning very rapidly. Now notice what direction it is spinning. Imagine that the pinwheel is glowing in the color you associate with stress.
4. Change the color of stress to the color that you associate with relaxation and feeling at peace. Begin to make the pinwheel or windmill slow down, until its spinning stops. Then slowly reverse the direction, so it is turning slowly the opposite way. Continue to see or feel it turn in that direction.

Now write your answers to these four questions.

What color do I associate with stress? _____

What color do I associate with feeling relaxed? _____

Which direction did the pinwheel or windmill spin in when I thought of stress?

_____

Which direction did I associate with relaxation? _____

REMEMBER,
if you can relax the mind,
your body will follow.

The "Step Away from Stress" Exercise

1. Stand up and shake out the tension in your arms and legs, then let your arms rest at your side. Take a few slow, gentle breaths.

2. Imagine that you are letting the stress leave your body as you exhale all the air out of your lungs, making an audible "hah!" sound.

3. Imagine that your nervousness or feeling of being stressed is a bubble or a balloon floating beside you. Make it the color you associate with stress.

4. Take a giant step away from this bubble or balloon, then walk away a few more steps, as if you could leave the stress behind you.

5. Walk about in a calm and confident manner, smiling to yourself. Tell yourself that you are "feeling good."

We have just gone through instructions for exercises that help you relax, so you can calm yourself down and manage the internal distraction of anxiety. When you feel less anxious and more in control, it is much easier to focus on your skating and execute your elements well. When you feel less anxious and can focus, you can get yourself into your music for your program and bring out more of the artistic aspects of your skating, so feeling less anxious inside helps you focus on personal best skating, both technically and artistically.

It also helps to keep making sure that your muscles can "UN-tense" after you have been sitting for a long time or have been thinking about something that upsets you. We recommend that you occasionally check your posture and deliberately relax your shoulders and do a few neck rolls, very slowly.

If you can relax
your body,
your mind will follow.

❧ *Techniques for Decreasing Anxiety about Competitors and Increasing Your Capacity to Focus*

We have talked about what really defines personal best skating. It essentially means skating for your own reasons, focusing on your own skating, and comparing your yourself to your own progress of becoming more skilled in skating. When you focus on yourself and how you are skating, you are paying attention to what you can control. As we have suggested, you cannot completely control how the judges decide on placements, and you cannot control how your competitors, will perform.

Personal best skating focuses you away from comparing yourself to other skaters because this can be a huge source of anxiety for you or anyone else who is caught up in comparisons. Objective comparisons, such as reviewing the elements and artistic components in last year's winning long program, can be useful, especially as you and your coach are planning your programs for the upcoming season. At almost any other time, however, thinking about how much better or worse someone skates than you distracts you from your lesson or practice. The comparison—no matter if you see yourself as better or worse than the other skater—takes you off focus. Dwelling on how much better you are than others can detract from the process of improving your own ability. Because skating is such as challenging sport, even Olympians can enhance their skill and artistic ability. Chances are, so can you, even when you're winning—by focusing on what you're doing.

Comparing yourself unfavorably to another skater usually sets off anxiety because the comparison triggers negative thinking. Negative, pessimistic thoughts trigger feelings of being scared, worried, and distressed. Negative, pessimistic thoughts interfere with performing well. Thinking about competitors as people better than you usually makes you feel pretty miserable about yourself.

How do you stay out of comparisons? By making your comparisons more objective and by working toward that objective approach, you usually feel less upset about not skating as well as your goals specified. You can depersonalize, or objectify, competitors at your level by imagining an objective role model who does everything called for in the rule book, who skates artistically, and who loves to perform.

Some coaches call this objective role model the "phantom skater," like a masked character whose actual identity is not known. This way, you can set your goals in comparison to this phantom skater's achievements and then challenge yourself to meet that level of achievement *for yourself.*

How else can you get yourself out of comparisons? By purposefully putting your attention on your goals, your programs, your music, and your progress in every lesson and practice. You can stay away from comparisons by developing your capacity to focus, one of the most crucial mental training skills. You can pull your mind away from a counterproductive "I am less than ..." comparison by deliberately telling yourself to focus on *you* and what you are working on at that moment.

Even if we cannot completely get comparisons out of our thoughts, we can shift our attention away from upsetting and distracting comparisons to self-directed messages like "Pay attention to this moment. Skate for *you* in this moment."

In the next few pages, I will take you through the instructions for becoming more aware of what and how you are thinking. I will teach you specific techniques for focusing, ones used by elite and Olympic athletes in skating and other highly mental sports like gymnastics, golf, and martial arts.

～ *Directing Your Thinking to Create Your Personal Best Skating Performance*

IMAGINATION EXERCISES

Recall that we said that not everyone imagines in the same way. But everyone can develop his or her imagination, and thereby create desired mental performances in the mind. Imagining a good performance in your mind helps your body be better able to create it more accurately and quickly as you learn and practice the physical skills of skating. We can acquire a new element more effectively when we have deliberately imagined accomplishing that element correctly in our minds, either seeing it or feeling it. Try these next few exercises, and rate how vividly you hear, see, feel, taste, or smell what is suggested by using the following rating scale:

Write the number 1 if your imagination is very real.

Write the number 2 if your imagination is moderately real.

Write the number 3 if your imagination is somewhat real.

Write the number 4 if you cannot imagine the stimulus at all.

Rate your imagination on each stimulus using the scale on the previous page:

- [ ] Feel yourself kicking a soccer ball straight ahead.
- [ ] See the inside of your bedroom at home and notice where the furniture is.
- [ ] Feel yourself petting a gentle, friendly golden retriever.
- [ ] Hear the sound of thunder on a stormy afternoon.
- [ ] Taste an orange slice in your mouth.
- [ ] See a blank computer screen.
- [ ] Feel warm gloves on your hands.
- [ ] Hear the sound of your best friend's voice giving you a compliment.
- [ ] See a birthday cake with your name on it sitting on a table in front of you.
- [ ] Hear the sound of a cat purring.
- [ ] Taste chocolate cream pie on your tongue.
- [ ] Smell the scent of a rose.
- [ ] Feel yourself rotating in the air while executing a jump.
- [ ] Smell the scent of the ice rink where you practice.
- [ ] Hear the sound of the Zamboni making ice.
- [ ] Feel a gentle spring breeze on your cheek.
- [ ] Taste a scrambled egg. Feel its texture in your mouth.
- [ ] See a videotape of you skating well at a competition, a test, or an exhibition.
- [ ] Feel yourself lifting a watering can filled to the brim.
- [ ] See fireworks in a dark night sky.
- [ ] Feel yourself walking up very steep steps.
- [ ] Hear the sound of a car's engine starting.

Overall, how would you say you did on this imagination exercise?

THE MENTAL LOCKER

This next exercise is called by many different names, such as "the mental locker," "compartmentalizing," and "putting your cares away." Its purpose is to help you clear internal mental distractions in the form of any thought, positive or negative, that is unrelated to your skating. This exercise helps you focus better because you are deliberately setting thoughts aside that interfere with putting your full mental attention on your skating. When your full mental attention is on your skating, you can be more fully involved in your skating in a physical sense, too.

The Mental Locker Exercise

1. Sit or lie down comfortably in a place that is quiet and where you won't be disturbed.
2. Gently close your eyes and breathe in a slow, rhythmic manner. If you like, you can follow the pacing sequence, "breathe in—pause—breathe out" for one or two minutes.
3. Picture a locker like you would see in a school hallway, or imagine a container that is yours for storing distracting thoughts when you want to focus on skating. You can use the school locker or create a container like a box, jar, or trunk in which to store thoughts unrelated to skating. Make sure that this container has a lid. If you are using the mental locker, make sure it has a door that closes completely.
4. Think about the program you are working on with your coach. If you don't currently have a program, think about an element that you are learning in your lessons.
5. Keep your mind focused on these skating thoughts as clearly as you can.
6. When you start to notice a thought that is unrelated to skating, imagine putting that thought into your container. Soon your container may become crowded with thoughts that have nothing to do with skating and that could be internal distractions interfering with your performance if you didn't set them aside quickly.
7. When you have stowed away the unrelated thoughts, go back to imagining yourself skating. What do you notice? Can you think about your skating more easily?
8. You can use this exercise each time you lace up your boots, in order to clear your mind for just skating. In this way you can be better focused.

Other Ways to Use the Mental Locker Exercise

As a sport psychologist, I often help athletes learn to manage those internal distractions called "worries." Worries can be about almost anything. Skaters can find themselves worrying about skating or worrying about other things going on in their lives, including situations they might call problems.

You can use the mental locker exercise any time you want to clear your mind of worry so you can better focus on the task at hand, whether it is your schoolwork, talking to a friend, or going out to have fun.

THE MENTAL ROOM

In the United States and in many other countries, sport psychologists teach Olympic hopefuls how to imagine and plan for optimal performance at the Games. One of the best-known mental training techniques taught to Olympians the world over is called the "mental room." It is such a helpful way to imagine yourself performing your personal best that I want to teach it to you here.

The mental room technique builds upon the imagination exercise that you learned on pages 50 and 51. In the mental room exercise, you construct a place that is yours alone, where you can go when you want to plan for and see/feel your desired performance. You can also use your mental room for reviewing your successful performances of the past or for recalling other happy times.

Mental Room Exercise

1. Sit down with your back straight and your head leaning against something, if possible. Place your hands, palms down, on your knees. Gently close your eyes.
2. Imagine creating in your mind a special place just for yourself, where you can go to plan or review successful performances and happy times.
3. Construct this room in your imagination. It can look like a real room or it can be a place in a location you make up, like a virtual world or space.
4. Furnish your mental room comfortably in a way that pleases you. Create a chair to sit in that is facing a big projection screen. You can imagine the screen like a giant television screen or like the one you see in a movie theater.

5. In one hand you are holding a remote control. Imagine that you can use it to direct the play back of images on the screen that let you re-live past successful performances in your skating or any other happy time you want to recall.

6. See yourself on the screen skating well in some past performance you were pleased with. Really notice the details of your moving around the ice.

7. Now see yourself enjoying a past happy time in some activity other than skating. Make this imagining as vivid as you can on the screen.

8. Imagine that you can project onto the screen images of what you want to do in your skating. You can picture yourself landing a jump that you have been working on or executing an element very well.

You can use this movie screen anytime to view yourself getting ready for a test day or competition, and to see yourself skating well in that test or competition. You can visit this mental room any time it would cheer you up to think about things in skating that you have done well.

This success review of positive past events is a powerful way that athletes get themselves out of discouragement, and is a method for recovering mentally from a loss or disappointment.

Use the space below to draw a picture of your mental room.

∾ *Improving Your Health*

It is important to improve your general health so that being ill is not an internal distraction for your skating (and so you just feel better!).

What was the date of your last physical exam with your doctor? _____

Did the doctor discover at that time that you had any health problems? If no, that's

great. If yes, what were they? _____

How are you taking care of these health problems? _____

_____

Other Lifestyle Factors Linked to Staying Healthy and How Thinking Affects Your Health

On pages 30–32 I talked about the benefits for your skating of thinking optimistically. Something else Dr. Martin Seligman discovered from his research was that people who learned to think more optimistically actually had fewer communicable illnesses like colds and flu. This is a remarkable finding because it means that pessimistic thinking actually has an adverse impact on your immune system, the body's natural set of defenses against illness.

So catching your pessimistic thoughts and switching them to more optimistic thoughts will help your health as well as your skating!

What else can you do to stay healthy? Getting enough sleep is important, not just to avoid the internal distraction of sleep deprivation but to protect your physical well-being. Taking a rest period after a skating session in which you really pushed yourself is also helpful, to allow your energy to be restored.

Pace yourself when you have a lot to do, whether it's at your job, or with your schoolwork. Planning ahead for a major project helps you feel more in control, since you can avoid the last-minute rushing around and perhaps some stress as well.

⟲ Learning To Manage Negative Emotions Like Fear, Anger, Or Feeling Overwhelmed

On the last several pages, you learned several strategies for managing internal distractions like anxiety and worry and also ways to calm down physical symptoms like a rapid heartbeat. There are also other techniques for helping you calm down when you are feeling fearful, angry, or overwhelmed.

We have already talked about three of the symptoms of negative emotions: rapid heartbeat, irregular breathing, and tense muscles. There are other symptoms of negative emotions that it will be helpful for you to understand and learn to manage— cold hands and feet, butterflies in the stomach or even nausea, dizziness, dry mouth, shakiness or trembling, a narrowing of peripheral vision, and feeling "strange."

All these symptoms are part of the automatic response set known as "fight or flight." When we think we are in danger of either being hurt or shamed and embarrassed, a hormone known as adrenalin (epinephrine) is released, affecting many of the body's systems. Adrenalin prepares the body to cope with the perceived danger by either running away (the flight part) or fending off the attacker (the fight part).

This fight or flight response is exactly what we need when we are truly in danger; for example, if we are about to be run over as we step from the curb, or someone suspicious approaches us. We won't have to think about jumping back from the car or running from the unsavory-looking person while screaming for help. The body acts automatically to get out of harm's way.

Adrenalin is thus really our friend; certainly it is part of our human evolutionary system that helped our ancestors survive, and it helps us, too.

All these symptoms don't feel so great on a test day or at a competition when we are nervous or worried that we will perform well. Remember, if a skater has winning as her outcome goal, she perceives that looking good is really important and that falling is a catastrophe. Her mind will send her body an interesting message that goes something like this, "Help, this is a life or death matter! I am in danger! If I don't win, I will die of embarrassment! And I can't make the judges do what I want!" At that point, the skater can be looking for the exit, or running to the bathroom to relieve herself of her lunch, or trembling with fear.

What can help her with these awful physical symptoms? First, she could shift her goal from an outcome goal that she can't totally control to a performance goal over which she has more control. She can think about skating as one part of her life, not the only thing. And she can prepare to get up quickly, smiling, if she falls.

What are the ideas here that could work for *you*? First, when we are truly in danger, we want the fight or flight response to help us stay alive. When we are fearful but not in actual physical danger, we can reconfigure how we look at the situation that provokes our fear. By this act, we keep the situation, like skating, in perspective. Optimistic thinking helps: there is a tomorrow, another lesson, and another practice. There is even another season if we are worrying about qualifying for Divisional competition. There is even another way to skate. If a skater finds he is not able to master technical elements well enough to advance in competitive skating, he could consider focusing on artistic programs, skating in exhibitions, or ice dancing.

Describe a fear-triggering thought you once had during a test day or competition.

_____

_____

_____

Rewrite it, bringing in a more fear-reducing optimistic perspective.

_____

_____

_____

How could this new thought have helped you feel more comfortable that day?

_____

_____

_____

OTHER TECHNIQUES FOR MANAGING FEAR

- Make yourself more comfortable—wrap yourself up in a blanket or comforter and sit in a quiet place. In this environment listen to soothing music, perhaps classical, or to tapes of nature sounds.
- Talk over the fear with a person whom you trust—a parent, your coach, an older and wiser person, or your minister, rabbi, or priest.
- Write about what is making you fearful. Read it to the person you trust.
  If you have a fear about your health or an injury, talk this over with your doctor.
- Read something that is inspirational.
- Read stories about the courage of ordinary people doing extraordinary things.

If there is someone who is provoking your fear, decide what action you might take to get this person to stop. This could mean talking to the administrators at your school or to your school counselor, talking to the director of the rink if someone there is behaving badly, or reporting the person to the police. Get help from the person you trust in deciding what to do. Then allow this trusted person to assist you in taking action.

Remember, we can divide our fear and take steps to overcome it by sharing our worries with someone who cares about our well-being.

If you are currently grappling with a fear about skating or something else, list the things you can do to help yourself manage it or even change the situation that is provoking it. _____

_____

_____

_____

_____

_____

_____

TECHNIQUES FOR COPING WITH ANGER

It helps to understand that fear may lead to anger if we feel that something important to us is being threatened. We can also feel angry if someone is teasing us or undermining us. Anger can quickly trigger the fight or flight response if we feel we are not being treated with respect. It really helps to know techniques for managing the physical symptoms of anger and to be prepared to communicate assertively with the person who is the source of our anger.

Empowering Visualizations

You can imagine yourself as strong as an oak or cypress tree, with deep roots that hold you firmly as you handle difficulty. Imagine you are wise so you can see with more perspective. You can also reconnect to a feeling of inner strength by remembering a time in your skating when you felt you skated strong and well, and were so involved in your skating that you were almost unaffected by competitors. (This is another example of the "Success Review" technique described on page 39).

1. Slow your breathing down to calm you and steady you.
2. Count to ten before taking any action, unless your anger is being triggered by something that is putting you in actual danger.
3. Walk away from a situation that is making you angry. Taking a time-out can give you some distance and a few minutes to calm your physical symptoms, to get your perspective back, and to decide what response is your best.
4. Get assistance in dealing with the person who is provoking your anger.

Speak Up Using Assertive Communication Skills

There are four steps for coping with anger outlined in the book *Asserting Yourself: A Practical Guide for Positive Change* by Sharon and Gordon Bower. Describing what is upsetting you is step one. Expressing your feelings to the person at whom you are angry is the next step. Step three is specifying what you want to see the other person change. The fourth step is telling the person with whom you are angry what consequences will occur—positive ones if he makes the change, or negative consequences if he doesn't.

It is beyond the scope of this book to teach this useful communication tool of speaking assertively when you are angry. You may be able to find an assertive communication class at school or through your community's university extension program.

These skills are most effective when practiced with a trainer and when tailored to meet the situation that is upsetting.

What we can teach you here are some communication skills for talking to yourself when you are feeling angry, afraid, or overwhelmed. These skills allow you to be your own internal coach and prepare you for a stressful event like being around competitors who are trying to psych you out. This internal-coach technique allows you to steady yourself when you face something difficult like unkind remarks from another skater's parents or coach.

This self-talk communication skill set, stress inoculation training (SIT) was developed by Donald Meichenbaum, a psychologist. Stress inoculation was named after the medical procedure of inoculation, meaning vaccinating a person against disease—like getting a flu shot so you won't get the flu during the flu season. In the same way, SIT vaccinates you against stress so you won't get as upset or off track when you face a situation. SIT prepares you to cope effectively and stay strong in your response.

How To Use Stress Inoculation Training (SIT)

1. Think of a stressful skating situation that you have encountered and may deal with again in the future. Most skaters come up with situations involving competitors or competitors' parents, friends, or coaches. They often recall something that has happened at an earlier competition that was difficult for them. Now think about what you did then and what happened next.

Write down the situation that happened to you and describe what you did and what happened next. _____

_____

_____

_____

_____

_____

_____

2. Think about what you could have done to prevent the situation from occurring. One possibility is to avoid the people or to walk away when they start to say something mean.

Write down an idea for what you might have done to have prevented the situation you described above from happening.

_____

_____

_____

_____

3. Sometimes preventing a situation is impossible—it happens before you can think about getting away from it. In this case, it is important to do something right then to keep the situation from getting worse. One idea is to get help from your coach or parents to respond to the person who is being difficult. Another idea is to say something back.

Write down what you could have done in the situation to have kept things from getting worse. _____

_____

_____

_____

4. Think about how you would prepare yourself to capably handle this same situation in the future.

Write down what you would do beforehand. _____

_____

_____

_____

Write down what might get really tough and how you would handle that, either on your own or by getting help. _____

_____

_____

_____

5. Stress inoculation training not only includes these preparation steps, but the use of internal-coach statements that you say to yourself before, during, and after a stressful situation.

Look at this list of internal-coach statements. They are divided up into categories of before, during, and after a stressful event. In our experience, the statements below have been most helpful to skaters who are facing tough situations with competitors or other people in the rink.

Before Statements
"What do I have to do in this situation?"
"Just stay focused on what I can do to cope."
"I have a plan for dealing with this."

Choose one of these "before" statements that you think might help you if you encounter the situation you are considering here in the future, or think of one of your own. Write it here. _____

_____

During Statements
"Take a deep breath and try to relax. I can stay in control of my response to this."
"I can handle this."
"Don't take his(her) words personally."
"As long as I stay cool-headed, I am more in control."
"One step at a time."

Choose one of the "during" statements that you think might help you in this situation in the future, or think of one of your own. Write it here.

After Statements

"That was pretty good, given how stressed out I've been about this."

"Good. I did it. Next time, I'll do even better."

"I handled it OK."

Choose one of these "after" statements that you think might help you in your situation in the future, or think of one of your own. Write it in the space below.

There is one additional category of internal-coach statement. These help a skater cope and keep going when he or she experiences a setback. The examples below are ones we chose because they seem to work the best for skaters.

Coping With Setbacks Statements

"Rest and figure out what to do next."

"Everybody has a setback. This is mine. I can fix what didn't work for me
          and come back strong."

"Focus on my progress, not perfection."

"I can get past this disappointment. I get another chance."

Choose one of these coping statements that you think might help you in a setback situation in the future, or think of one of your own. Write it here.

✑ *Coping with a Current Skating Injury*

In our chapter in *Skate Your Personal Best* on conditioning, Donna Burden, the USFSA Physical Therapist for the 1998 Winter Olympics, talks about the ways to avoid injuries. To summarize here:

- Warm up properly first before getting on the ice.
- Learn the correct technique for a challenging element.
- Avoid an overuse injury, which can be caused by making too many attempts of one particular jump without rest in a practice session or lesson.
- Develop your flexibility and strength in an off-ice program where your training and conditioning needs have been evaluated.

Donna reminds skaters to listen to your body and to report soreness to your coach. Ask your coach's help in making an adjustment in what you are doing or leaving the ice altogether if it feels like you might be injured.

If you are injured now, what can you do to heal effectively and return to the ice in good shape? Follow the directions of your sport medicine physician or orthopedic specialist for staying off the ice and for any treatments (medications, exercises) you require. Follow the rehabilitation plan given to you by your physical therapist, if your doctor has put you in the care of another professional.

Write here what your rehabilitation plan is for recovering from your injury.

_____

_____

_____

_____

_____

_____

_____

What Else Helps In Healing An Injury?

Talk over what this injury means to your skating season with the professional caring for you (like the physical therapist you are seeing regularly) and your coach.

Who are the people with whom you have discussed your injury?

_____

_____

What have you concluded your injury means to your skating for the rest of this season?_____

_____

Spend time with people who are supportive of you as a whole person, and not just as a skater.

Who are your support people?_____

_____

When did you last spend time with them? _____

Plan your comeback to your normal skating schedule after you have recovered from your injury. This plan may involve several people: your doctor, your physical therapist, an athletic trainer, your coach, and your parents.

After talking with the people involved in your injury recovery, write out the plan for your return to your normal skating routine. _____

_____

_____

_____

Techniques for coping with negative emotions may help you cope with the frustration and upset of being injured and unable to skate as you normally do. These techniques are taught on pages 56–63.

Injury usually means that a skater has pain, from mild to severe, and requires therapeutic interventions such as medication. Professionals in the field of sport medicine have noted the importance of athletes knowing strategies for responding to the pain from injury. Many researchers have identified different strategies for coping with pain in general. If you are interested in reading their studies, see the reference section of *Skate Your Personal Best.*

Four Types of Mental Techniques
Research has found that four types of mental techniques work best with most pain patients. These techniques appear to help reduce a person's experience of pain by relaxing the muscles and decreasing the stress response to the pain.

We want to summarize these pain management strategies as possible ways you can help yourself when you are recovering from an injury and are off the ice for some time.

In the first technique, you turn your attention away from the pain to something else, like sitting outside and noticing the flowers and plants around you. You could also watch TV, listen to books on tape, or let yourself get caught up in music that you enjoy.

Write here what you could do to turn your attention to something external.

_____

_____

The second technique draws your attention away from the pain to something internal that is pleasant. On pages 45–46, you created a place in which you felt relaxed. You can use this technique and visit this place to manage pain as well. You can also just let your imagination go, and think about a person you like and spending time with him or her. In the research, this method was the most effective in helping people cope with their pain.

Write here what you could do to turn your attention to something internal that is

pleasant . _____

_____

_____

The third technique directs your thoughts to some activity that is just neutral, like organizing your desk or washing the car.

Write here what you could think about that is emotionally neutral.

_____

_____

_____

The final technique involves saying something to yourself or performing some mental activity in a rhythmic manner. You could recite a nursery rhyme in a monotone, or you could repeat an inspirational saying or positive statement in a solemn way, as if you were lecturing to an audience. Your mind's attention can be drawn away from pain by both the activity and the way in which you utter the words or numbers.

Write here the inspirational saying or positive statement that you could repeat to yourself in this manner. _____

_____

_____

These last two techniques might seem a little silly or boring. They do, however, offer a change of pace from the other techniques, and they grab your attention, even for a short while, when you have tired of imagining pleasant things or watching TV.

Preparing for Your Comeback to a Normal Skating Routine While Coping with the Fear of Reinjury

When a skater has been injured while on the ice, it is understandable that he or she would feel afraid of the same injury occurring again after resuming activity. If this fear is not addressed, the skater may delay returning to the ice, or he or she may avoid the element that was being attempted when the injury happened. A skater who was injured while jumping might find he hesitates on his takeoffs after returning to the ice, although he did not do this before his injury.

What can a skater do to manage the fear of reinjury?

If you have been injured on the ice and are preparing to come back, it is a good idea to talk about any concerns that you have about the possibility of the injury repeating itself. You can talk about the circumstances surrounding the injury and understand what happened and what you can do to keep it from occurring again. Both your coach and your physical therapist might be good to talk to about this. If you skate pairs, certainly talk about this with your partner so you can plan your injury prevention strategies together.

Write what the circumstances were in your skating injury here.

_____

_____

_____

After talking it over, write what your injury prevention strategies are here.

_____

_____

_____

_____

_____

Write any techniques for managing fear as you come back here.

_____

_____

_____

Techniques for Coping with Fatigue

Fatigue or tiredness is a natural result of physical exertion, and mentally taxing activities, as well as of stressful situations that have continued for days or weeks, or sleep deprivation. On pages 40–42 we talk about identifying when you are not getting enough sleep and taking steps to remedy this situation. We have also recommended that you take naps and that you rest after particularly intense practice sessions. Several techniques for relaxing yourself to better cope with stress are presented on pages 42–48.

We encourage you to take care of yourself so fatigue can be prevented naturally.

What can you do if you are feeling tired and have a test to skate or a qualifying competition in two hours? Here are some ideas for energizing yourself when there is no time to sleep or even nap. The following techniques can help you get psyched up. These techniques are not meant to replace the sleep and rest you must have, so please use them with care.

1. When feeling droopy, jog in place for two minutes to elevate your heart rate.
2. Listen to fast, upbeat music. Music used in aerobics classes can be invigorating.

Write the name below of the fast-paced music that wakes you up.

_____

_____

_____

3. Use your imagination to recall a time when you felt you had great energy and went on to perform with intensity and finished strong without being too tired.

Write about the skating situation in which you felt great energy here.

_____

_____

_____

_____

_____

4. Use pump-up phrases that you shout out loud like: "Let's go!" "Move it!" "Push!" "You can do it!" "Energize!"

Or write your own pump-up phrases here.

_____

_____

_____

_____

5. Some skaters like to use their imagination to think about the feeling of a sleek animal that possesses great energy, like a cheetah or galloping horse. They imagine how quickly this animal moves about in order to get themselves up to skate. This may appeal to you.

If so, write the name of that animal here. _____

6. What you are eating can also affect whether you feel energized or sluggish. We discuss the effects of food on mood and energy levels in our book, *Skate Your Personal Best*. Here we just want to suggest that you may feel less fatigued if you eat a small meal that contains protein. You could try a sandwich made with chicken or tuna. You could mix protein powder in lowfat milk or juice. You could have a hard boiled egg on toast. Protein can help improve your sense of mental alertness, which can influence how fatigued you feel when you are actually physically tired.

External Distractions

Skaters may encounter a sense of having too much to do, especially during the competition season. This feeling may be experienced as worry about meeting deadlines and not being able to accomplish everything that needs to be done. Internally, the feeling of being overwhelmed can feel like anxiety, with a rapid heartbeat and difficulty focusing. To manage this internal feeling, a skater must first look at the circumstances outside herself that are causing the overwhelmed feeling—what psychologists call "external distractions." These externals distractions may interfere with focusing if a skater worries that there are too many things to do and thinks about those things rather than skating.

Below is a list of important things in life other than skating. Sometimes these parts of life present problems for skaters and become external distractions. Sometimes, life is going well but a skater is busier than she can comfortably handle and feels overwhelmed.

Look at the list below. Some of these aspects of life will be relevant for you, while others will not. Think carefully about which ones, if any, may be operating as external distractions in your life right now. In the context of skating, an external distraction would mean a part of your life that is problematic or so busy that you cannot focus well on your skating and your thoughts keep drifting to that part of your life instead.

Check The External Distractions That Are a Problem for You

- [ ] Home situation—how well my family is getting along.
- [ ] Home situation—any outside problems my family is facing.
- [ ] Home situation—any health problems my family is facing.
- [ ] Home situation—brothers and sisters and their problems.
- [ ] Finances—enough money for skating?
- [ ] Finances—other money worries?
- [ ] School—are my grades a concern? Am I keeping up with the work?
- [ ] Friends—am I having a conflict with a friend?
- [ ] Friends—do I have enough time to spend with friends outside of skating?
- [ ] Special person in my life—do I have enough time with him or her?
- [ ] Special person in my life—are we getting along?
- [ ] Job—am I doing OK with my co-workers and boss?
- [ ] Problems at the rink (other skaters or their coaches or parents).

Even though the previous checklist is helpful, please also write the specific external distractions that are affecting you right now and interfering with your ability to focus.

_____

_____

_____

_____

∽ Managing External Distractions

To help manage the feeling of being overwhelmed, first see if you can identify which situation needs fixing right now. An example might be: "My parents are upset that my grades in school have dropped since I started skating ten more hours per week."

Write that situation here. _____

_____

_____

_____

When we let ourselves analyze what is distracting and overwhelming us, we start the process of taking charge. When we define what is going on, we get less confused. When we figure out if there is any action we can take to fix a situation, we are acting as if what we do matters. If we take some action to fix something, we feel less helpless.

If you can solve a problem, your life will probably feel like it works better, and you can focus more on your skating when you are on the ice. Here are the steps you can take to try and make a situation in your life better.

We go through these steps using the example, "My parents are upset that my grades in school have dropped since I started skating ten more hours per week."

Use your situation from above for working through the steps.

Step 1. Ask yourself: what is the problem I am having in the situation? Be as specific as you can be.

In our example, the problem could be stated as:

> My parents are upset with me, and that's a problem because I want to get along with them. My grades have dropped, and that's a problem because I want to go to college and grades influence where I can be admitted. I am skating more now to prepare for competitions because I need more hours on the ice in order to be ready. But that's a problem because I am not finishing my homework; and since I'm not turning it in, my grades are falling.

Write your explanation of your problem here. _____

_____

_____

_____

Step 2. Get information about the problem so you can really understand what is actually going on.

Using our example:

> I could get more information about the problem by talking to my parents, teachers, and coach. I might find out that my teachers think I am a good student and are wondering why I am suddenly not getting my homework in on time. My parents may be concerned and not just angry with me. My coach may also be concerned and willing to change the practice schedule.

Write what kind of information you could gather about your problem here. Set a

date for obtaining this information. _____

_____

_____

_____

_____

Date _____

Step 3. Get help from people involved in the problem, if you can.

In the example, the skater could ask for help as she went about seeking more information about the problem. She could ask her parents, her teachers, and coach to assist her in finding a solution to the problem.

Write the names of the people you could ask for help here.

_____

_____

_____

_____

Step 4. With the helpful input of the other people whom you have named, think of possible solutions to the problem.

In the example:

The skater found out her parents wanted her to get her grades up as quickly as she could. They also realized that she was skating more and that she had less time for schoolwork. Her parents told her that they believed skating was less important than school but also recognized her desire to skate well and to be prepared to compete. One of her teachers said skating was a waste of time and simply wanted her to get back to work.

Another teacher, when told of the competition schedule, was willing to adjust some deadlines for two term papers because the skater had been doing well in the class. Her father agreed to drive the skater to the local library after the afternoon session so the skater could do homework there before returning to the rink for the final early evening practice. The skater's parents allowed her to continue skating the additional hours, on a trial basis of two weeks, on the condition that her homework had to be completed on time and that she receive at least a B on each assignment.

Write possible solutions to your problem here. _____

_____

_____

_____

Step 5. Implement the solution or solutions that make sense both to you and to the people you have asked for help. Give the solution sufficient time to see if it is working.

Write your solution(s) here. _____

_____

_____

_____

Specify the length of time that you will try out your solution. _____

Step 6. At the end of the time period, check to see how well your solution has worked. If it didn't work as well as you needed it to, talk again with the people helping you to find an alternative solution. Repeat steps 5 and 6.

In the example:

The skater found that some people in her life did not perceive her skating was as important as she felt it was. One of her teachers stood firm on the issue of turning homework in on time. With the other teacher, the skater found that a compromise was possible—that is, a resolution of the problem in which each side yields or gives up something to come to a solution. The skater also received assistance from her coach, who agreed to drive her to a place away from the rink where it was easier to get homework done.

In your information gathering about a difficult situation, you may find out several things. For example, you may not be able to change your family's financial situation. So, if you are older, you may need to find your own sources of money for your skating, perhaps by working at a part-time job. If you are a National competitor, you and your coach may want to find outside sponsorship for your skating. Your own actions may be necessary to help improve the situation.

If your problem was being bothered at the rink by a competitor, you may find out in your information gathering is that this skater practices on the same session you do. One solution to a problem may be to avoid the source of the difficulty. This can work sometimes, but at other times it is impossible without great sacrifice on your part.

Pretend you are the skater whose competitor makes unkind remarks to you and you must skate the same practice session. If you avoid this session, you will be sacrificing some important skating time. What else can you do?

You might first try to get the other person to change what he or she is doing. You could ask to speak with the person in private. You could try to find out how this situation got started from the other person's point of view. You could then ask the person to stop the behavior that is difficult for you. If you can persuade the other person to change, that's great.

Let's say the other person doesn't change, but you don't want to skip the skating session to avoid the unkind remarks. You may need to make some adaptation in how you handle the problem.

Adaptation can be internal, such as shifting your view of what is happening. You might decide that you won't personalize the person's remarks to you and will therefore, ignore them. If the person has not made any physical gesture toward you, perhaps this is an appropriate response.

Adaptation can also be outward by staying in the environment but behaving differently yourself. You might decide to talk to the other skater's coach with your coach present, requesting that the other coach intervene with the offending skater. If you are not satisfied with that result, you could devise your own internal response to the remarks— one that you say as unemotionally as possible. You might try, "Work on your own stuff." Or you could say, "Give it a rest," and go immediately back to what you are doing.

These problem-solving skills can help you better focus on skating and are useful in taking care of things unrelated to your skating.

Write down a problem you now face (or have faced in the past) in which avoiding a person might be a good solution to try. _____

_____

_____

_____

If this is a problem occurring now, you could try avoidance as a solution. Try this solution and come back to this page later.

Write about how well this solution worked for you. _____

_____

_____

_____

_____

_____

Write down a problem you face now (or have in the past) in which staying in the environment but changing your behavior might be a good solution to try.

_____

_____

_____

_____

If this is a problem occurring now, you could try changing your behavior as a solution. Try this solution and come back to this page later.

Write about how well this solution worked for you.

_____

_____

_____

_____

_____

Write down a problem you now face (or have in the past) in which staying in the

environment but changing your behavior might be a good solution to try.

_____

_____

_____

_____

If this is a problem occurring now, you could try changing your behavior as a solution. Try this solution and come back to this page later.

Write about how well this solution worked for you.

_____

_____

_____

_____

_____

_____

_____

Two More Exercises to Help You Practice Focusing on One Thing and Manage External Distractions Like Unrelated Thoughts

Exercise One

Directions: Find someone to help you with this exercise. Have the other person select one alphabet letter that you will search for among the jumbled letters below. Have the person time you for one minute after telling you the letter to look for and giving you a "go!" signal. As you look for each one of the, let's say, Ps, have the other person try to distract you verbally by calling out the names of other letters. Ask the other person not to shout and to refrain from touching you. The point here is for him or her to distract you by just saying the names of other letters. Try to stay as focused as you can on what you are supposed to be doing. You can repeat this exercise several times with various letters.

A N Z R T L F P S D G W T Y I Q
Y B X S F K I E S P A N Z V U H E
B T O W V K D Y S O M R U A Z
K I X D G T R P Q A M J S L F Y
U T R S P H D C N L W U F N I T
R J A N C O S R P F K Q U T I B V
L W O Y C Z V I Q P L S K T R M
H T S P O L W U E M C I O Q N
V M K Q U E F A L J Z C N V B Y S
T D G P L W E M U S G J D Y F U I
D J H V N Q Y P O L S U J A S B M
M W I T O C N S G J S K F C X Q X

Exercise Two

Directions: Have another person time you for one minute. See how quickly you can connect the dots in order from 1 to 100 while the other person is singing or trying to distract you with unrelated conversation. Focus as well as you can on your task at hand and see if you can screen out the distraction the other person is making.

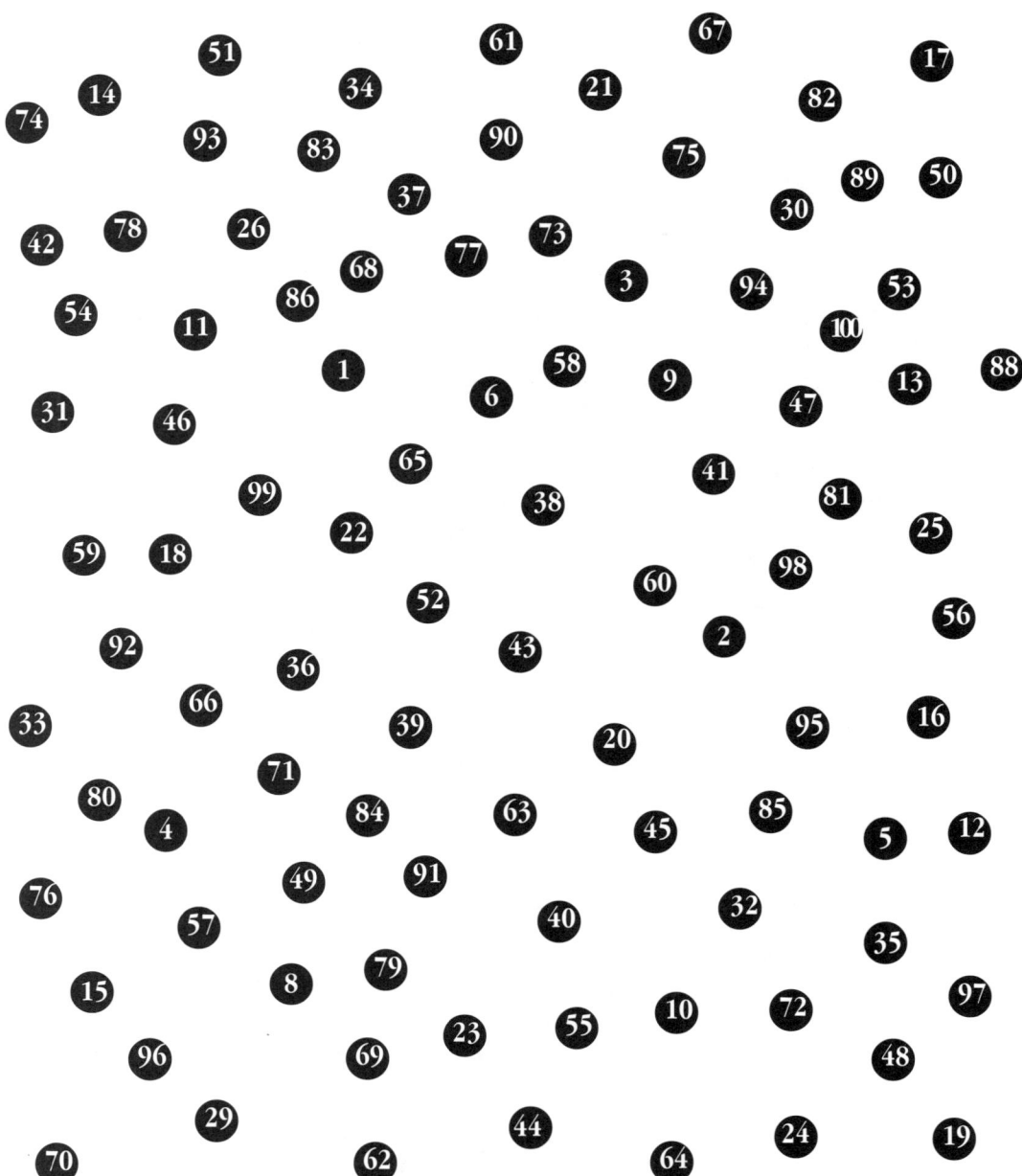

Techniques For Focusing

Now that you know how to manage internal and external distractions you are better able to focus.

ᨏ *Centering Physically*

Stand with your feet about shoulder-width apart. Close your eyes. Notice where you feel the center of your body. Is it your stomach (like your navel)? Is it the area around your heart? Is it your gut (abdomen)?

*Write here where you experience the center of your body.*_____

ᨏ *Centering "Key Word"*

You can use a special key word to draw your focus back into your body when you have become distracted. Skaters and other athletes use words like *balanced* or *centered* or *get quiet.* You can also make up your own key word.

Write your centering key words here. _____

ᨏ *Bring Yourself into the Present Moment*

As we have said, it helps you to focus on what you can control, like what is going on *now*, instead of worrying about the future or rehashing the past. Key words like *now* or *present moment* or *be here* can help you get back into the present.

You can also use the focusing question that has helped many skaters we have worked with: "What am I supposed to be doing right now?"

Write here what your key words or phrase for bringing yourself back to the present.

_____

ᨏ *Using a Key Word to Focus on Your Performance Task at Hand*

You can use a key word or phrase that puts your mind's attention on how you can execute an element. An example for a double jump could be *pull in tight.*

Write an example of a key word here. _____

Conditioning for Skating Excellence and Injury Prevention

The importance of off-ice conditioning for figure skaters was addressed at the International Congress on Medicine and Science in Figure Skating, which convened at the 1997 World Championships in Lausanne, Switzerland. A set of recommendations was issued, and we want to summarize them for you. Donna Burden's recommendations described in *Skate Your Personal Best* are consistent with these.

Finding the right off-ice conditioning program for a skater is a highly individual matter. Even when following the recommendations listed below, a skater should work with his coach to locate a professional who can design a program to fit his age, stage of growth, skating level, and current physical condition. We cannot prescribe the specifics that such a program would entail, but what we do in the next few pages is to share the international skating community's view with you. Then we will share the basics of Donna's suggestions for warming up, cooling down, and stretching. These are meant as suggestions only. Please review any off-ice conditioning with your coach and trainer.

The consensus of the gathering in Lausanne was that off-ice training was helpful to skaters in general and should be done to prepare skaters to participate in the sport. Off-ice training was crucial for the areas of physiological development necessary for skating safely and well: balance, flexibility, coordination, strength, and cardiovascular capacity.

Off-ice conditioning activities can be designed to help skaters advance in these areas and can also be tailored to help develop specific elements such as jumps and pair moves. Off-ice conditioning should be periodized, which means that activities correspond to different phases of the competitive skating season to help the skater be fit and prepared—but not overtrained—by the time that qualifying competitions get underway.

Off-ice conditioning was also viewed as important in the prevention of injuries to the soft tissues like muscles. Specially designed off-ice activities were also deemed important in recovery from a skating injury.

These are important guidelines for all skaters. Your coach can assist you in finding the right people to help you put your off-ice program together. You may also want to consider ballet classes for developing flexibility, coordination, and balance. Cross-training in other sports may be important to you as well. Ask your coach or the professional with whom you already work about the possible benefits of your participation in other athletic activities.

Write what you currently do for off-ice training here. If you don't have a program, write about what you want to discuss with your coach about starting one.

_____

_____

_____

List the activities that you plan to do for developing the following areas during this next skating year:

Flexibility _____

_____

Strength _____

_____

Aerobic capacity _____

_____

Coordination and balance _____

_____

Other off-ice activities that will help you with specific elements such as jumps or pair moves _____

_____

WARMING UP

Off-ice conditioning includes activities that help skaters feel ready to step on the ice. The first is warming up, something Donna Burden tells skaters they must do each time before they skate. Donna defines warming up as raising the core body temperature high enough to break a sweat. She notes that warming up is crucial in the morning but is also important before the afternoon sessions.

She says that the minimum time you should engage in warming up exercises is fifteen minutes, although the standard time is thirty minutes. She says that jumping rope is her preferred form of exercise and suggests that ten minutes be spent this way. The remainder of the time could be spent using an exercycle or slideboard, climbing stairs, bench stepping, or doing jumping jacks.

The warm-up should be followed by ten minutes of stretches. The purpose of stretching (to summarize Donna's words) is to lengthen the muscles after reclining in bed all night, to bring your attention to your muscles before you skate, and to prevent injury during practice or lessons. Donna reminds skaters that these ten minutes will not be sufficient to develop the flexibility that allows skaters to get the range of motion or extension they need in order to do incredible spirals and other moves, but the warm-up stretches are crucial for safe skating.

The cool-down after the last skating session could include finishing the session with some final stroking around the rink. After leaving the ice, Donna recommends completing the cool-down with some jogging in place or cycling on an exercycle.

While Tracy, Donna, and I all want to emphasize the importance of obtaining good professional assistance in designing your off-ice conditioning program, we can recommend a book of stretches and will illustrate the "functional" stretches you can do at home or at the rink. The book is entitled *The New York City Ballet Workout,* and it illustrates stretches for developing the flexibility that will enhance your figure skating. After carefully reviewing each stretch, Donna suggests that you omit one of them, the Stacked Hamstring and Calf stretch, because it will be difficult for most skaters to do correctly.

To be effective, Donna recommends that the muscle you are stretching be isolated so that the particular target area is actually the one receiving the benefit of stretching. She says that a good stretch must be held from two to five minutes. She cautions that the stretch should be one that is felt by the skater but that it shouldn't hurt.

The stretches on the next page are those you can do while watching TV at home at the end of the day. The first two are the familiar splits. The third one is a stretch for improving the turned-out position in ballet and skating. You can put a light-weight object over your crossed feet, such as a pillow, for a better stretch.

Remember, if a stretch hurts, stop!

The stretches we have illustrated are those which are beneficial for developing the flexibility that skaters need to skate their best and prevent injuries.

Before you turn to the stretches, we'd like to again emphasize the importance of warming up and stretching before each lesson and practice. If you are not doing this consistently, we would like to help you develop this consistency of warming up.

After consulting with your coach, please write down the warm-up activities and the time allocated for each that you will do before your first morning skate.

Activity _____ *Time allocation* _____ *minutes*

Activity _____ *Time allocation* _____ *minutes*

Activity _____ *Time allocation* _____ *minutes*

Activity _____ *Time allocation* _____ *minutes*

Activity _____ *Time allocation* _____ *minutes*

Activity _____ *Time allocation* _____ *minutes*

What can you do to make certain that you do your warm-up each morning?
An example might be to tell yourself "I am going to skate safely and my muscles will be more responsive if I do my warm-up."

Write what you can do or say to yourself to make sure you do your warm-up.

_____

_____

Is there anyone who can help you make certain you do your warm-up? An example might be to do your warm-up with a friend so you can encourage each other.

Write the name of that person here or any other idea for helping you do your

warm-up. _____

_____

ꙮ *Developing Cardiovascular Capacity on the Ice*

Many coaches recommend stroking classes for improving aerobic capacity. When you can move around the ice with speed for several minutes at a time, you are helping yourself prepare for skating your long program with enough breath for a strong finish.

One way to increase aerobic capacity is to skate at your top speed for the length of your long program. Before trying it, consult with your coach to see if these instructions need to modified in some way for you.

FUNCTIONAL STRETCHES FOR ATHLETES

Do these stretches for two-minute-minimum holds.

In split position, stretch chest to floor   *In split position, stretch nose to knee*

Relax on floor to obtain turned-out position

Fundamentals of Form and Control

IMPROVING YOUR POSTURE

As you watch yourself on videotape with your coach present, if possible, notice your posture as you skate. What do you like that you see about the way you hold your body and move across the ice?

What looks correct in terms of your form on the ice? _____

_____

_____

_____

What have you and your coach observed about your posture that you could improve?

_____

_____

_____

_____

What are the specific activities you can do to improve your posture?

_____

_____

_____

_____

Write any key words here that you can use while you skate in practice to remind yourself to skate with a strong back, head and arms up, and so on. _____

_____

_____

_____

Now notice on the videotape the extent to which you are skating under control. *What do you see that is working?*_____

_____

_____

_____

Is there any way in which you need to improve your sense of control as you skate?

_____

_____

_____

_____

☙ *Your Plan for Improving Your Sense of Skating Under Control*

Examples of a plan might be adding off-ice activities to help you with balance and coordination or taking an edge class to work on basic moves in the field. Decide with your coach what to do, and evaluate together what effects any special training has on your skating.

Sometimes a skater looks and feels out of control because he is not comfortable maneuvering about when other skaters are on the ice. Sometimes it is only practicing jumps when others are around that is unnerving for a skater, even for someone who is more advanced.

Tracy recommends that skaters move deliberately on the ice and use simple warnings such as "on your left" or "behind you." She strongly urges coaches to teach their younger skaters to get up off the ice quickly after falling and to hold their tears and upset for later, off the ice. Of course, if someone is injured, she suggests that those nearby skate away unless they are needed to help.

She recommends these strategies for using the ice well and being courteous to others without being overly uptight about sharing the ice with others.

1. Look ahead before attempting a jump. Use the ends of the rink. In some rinks, one end is designated as an area for jumping practice.

2. Indicate your intention by looking as if you are going to jump—have a determined look and a recognizable take-off position.

3. Look quickly to see if anyone has suddenly skated into your path.

4. If you fall, look around for someone approaching you as you get up quickly. Get yourself physically pulled together and mentally focused on what you are doing before making another attempt.

5. If you are really having an off-day and the rink is crowded, talk with your coach about practicing jumps during the next less-crowded session.

6. If you skate too close to someone, say something quickly like, "Excuse me."

7. If your miscalculated moves contribute to another skater's fall, stop and check to see if that person is OK. Apologize briefly.

8. If you collide with another skater, check if you are injured or if the other skater is hurt by the collision. If either of you is injured, request help from your coach, or from another person in charge if your coach is not present.

9. If you are really distracted by other skaters even if you know the rules for using the ice, focus more on *your* skating, especially getting down into the ice and feeling yourself moving. Let yourself be aware of what is happening near you while staying aware of your own moves. This gets better with practice.

10. If you are rattled by a past collision, let yourself be aware that your upset is understandable. Breathe as normally as you can and shake off the tension in your arms and legs every few minutes. Remind yourself that you can and will get past the upset about the collision and will enjoy your skating again soon.

Write any mental strategies which could help you feel more in control on the ice here, especially when the rink is crowded. _____

_____

_____

_____

Write any suggestions your coach has for you to better use the ice for improved comfort and control here. _____

_____

_____

_____

_____

_____

_____

_____

Spirals and Spins with Pizzazz

What are your goals for specific spirals for this skating season? _____

_____

_____

_____

What key words can help you learn and execute these elements more efficiently?

_____

_____

_____

What other activities can help you progress in developing spirals with pizzazz? (For example, you might do more stretching so your free leg can be lifted higher with greater ease.)

Write your ideas here. _____

_____

_____

_____

_____

_____

_____

_____

Write your goals for specific spins for this skating season here.

_____

_____

_____

_____

_____

_____

What key words can help you learn and execute these elements more efficiently?

_____

_____

_____

What other activities can help you progress in developing spins with pizzazz?
(An example might be more flexibility so you can get into your camel spin more easily.)

*Write your ideas here.*_____

_____

_____

_____

_____

_____

_____

Get Yourself Airborne—
Mastering Your Jumps

Write your goals here for specific jumps for this skating season.

_____

_____

_____

_____

STRATEGIES FOR LEARNING JUMPS

What key words or phrases can you use when you are practicing to help you learn your jumps more efficiently?

Jump _____ *Key word* _____

Jump _____ *Key word* _____

Jump _____ *Key word* _____

Jump _____ *Key word* _____

Jump _____ *Key word* _____

Jump _____ *Key word* _____

Jump _____ *Key word* _____

Jump _____ *Key word* _____

Jump _____ *Key word* _____

What other reminders from your coach could help you visualize and better feel each of the jumps that you are learning? _____

_____

_____

What jump that you are currently trying to learn is most challenging for you?

_____

Together with your coach, watch a videotape of your attempts. Discuss together what you need to change in order to get into the correct positions for take off, rotating, and landing. *Write those changes here.* _____

_____

_____

_____

What ideas can you use in feeling the correct position?

_____

_____

_____

_____

What were your coach's corrections? _____

_____

_____

_____

Strategies to Help You When You Have Difficulty Landing a New Jump

Discuss with your coach whether working in the harness would be helpful to you, if you have not yet already tried this learning aid.

What is a key word or phrase that can help you get into the correct position for this jump? "Be narrow" could be an example of a key phrase for a double Axel.

Write your key word or phrase here. _____

_____

If you are feeling anxious about this jump, think of some internal-coaching phrases you could say to yourself before your go into your take-off position. These statements should tell you what *to do*, and not what to avoid doing (not, "don't fall"). Two examples are "each try brings me closer" or "go after it!"

Write your internal-coaching statements here. _____

_____

_____

_____

Tracy has her skaters practice jumps in a sequence that makes sense for that skater. She limits the number of tries on any particular jump within a certain time period. Tracy does this to help a skater keep his frustration level down, and also to prevent an overtraining injury of the soft tissue.

If you have been working on a jump for some time and still haven't landed it, feeling upset and discouraged is understandable. If, however, your thinking is getting pessimistic at this point, you may be explaining your difficulty in terms like this: "I'll never get this jump." An attitude that bad things will last forever and that you will never get to your goal may reflect a pessimistic explanatory style.

Write a new optimistic statement to replace the pessimistic one.

An example might be, "I know I will eventually land this jump. Stay with it."

_____

_____

_____

Another pessimistic thought that can occur when you are having trouble with a jump is the spreading-negativity aspect of pessimism. This is when the skater says that the jump is not going well and neither are her spins. Then she says her footwork isn't so hot, either. And the rest of life is pretty awful, too.

Write a new optimistic statement to replace the pessimistic one.

An example could be "I know I'm having a tough time with this jump. But my other jumps are fine. My spirals are good. It's just this one jump."

_____

_____

_____

A third kind of pessimism is evident when the skater over-personalizes the problem with this jump. She explains her difficulty in the pessimistic explanatory style in this way: "I can't get it. It means I'm a lousy skater. I should just quit."

Write a new optimistic statement to replace the pessimistic one.

An example might be "This jump is hard for many people. When I have even a slightly off-day, my ability to get it right will be limited somewhat. I'm still a good skater."

_____

_____

_____

Off-Ice Techniques for Landing Jumps

Another technique is to visualize the jump first (or to imagine your best feeling of the jump if you don't visualize), then to step through it on the floor. If you have access to a gymnastics training facility, the "floor" is the padded area where gymnasts practice their floor exercises.

Some skaters imagine the jump and then simulate it in the "pit," an area dropped below the level of the "floor" and lushly padded with foam. Tracy has her skaters practice their jumps off the ice in just such a gymnastics facility. They also work on the trampoline to practice gaining height and getting precision in their rotations.

What can you do in off-ice activities to help you land your jumps?

_____

_____

_____

_____

_____

_____

_____

_____

_____

Developing Outstanding Programs

Planning Your Short (Technical) Program

What music are you using for your short program? _____

_____

These are the elements that must be included according to the USFSA rulebook:

_____

_____

_____

This becomes your objective comparison.

Last year's divisional (or national) winner at your level had these elements in his

or her program: _____

_____

_____

These are the details (footwork, arm, and hand positions, etc.) that you will be

including in your program: _____

_____

_____

_____

_____

Describe your costume for this program and paste in a picture of it below.

_____

_____

_____

_____

What is a key word or phrase that you could use for your short program?

_____

_____

_____

_____

PLANNING YOUR LONG (ARTISTIC) PROGRAM

What music are you using for your long program? _____

_____

What is the mood of your music? _____

_____

What is the meaning of your program or the story that it is conveying?

_____

_____

These are the elements that must be included according to the USFSA rulebook:

_____

_____

This becomes your objective comparison.

Last year's divisional (or national) winner at your level had these elements in his

or her program: _____

_____

_____

_____

These are the details (footwork, arm and hand positions, etc.) that you will be

including in your program: _____

_____

_____

Describe your costume for this program and paste a picture of it below.

_____

_____

_____

_____

What is a key word or phrase that you could use for your program?

_____

_____

_____

_____

Tracy helps her skaters refine their long programs by enlisting the help of a choreographer who works with the ballet teacher to instruct the skater in classical balletic positions and movements that enhance the artistic quality of that program. Discuss with your coach what resources you might use to improve the artistic aspects of your long program. Check below what points you want to refine, and name the people who might assist you in achieving the effect that you want.

Aspect Of Long Program   *Resource Person For Improvement*

Hand positions   _____

Arm positions   _____

Shoulder positions   _____

Toes turned out and pointed   _____

Head positions   _____

Neck positions   _____

Leg extensions (straight knees)   _____

Strong straight back while skating   _____

Facial expressions   _____

Write any other activities you can do to enhance the quality of your long program.
An example might be to practice program run-throughs (without jumps) on the floor in front of a mirror. _____

_____

_____

_____

_____

_____

Program Development Schedule
For Competitive Skaters

February	March	April	May	June	July
Search for music for competitive programs and make decisions. If skating in shows or exhibitions, prepare choreography for show program.	Edit music and prepare CD for competitive programs. Meet with choreographer. Complete choreography for competitive programs by late March. Design costumes. Meet with seamstress for fittings. Skate show program in shows and exhibitions. Junior Olympics Junior and Intermediate Peak Level	Clean the programs, adding any desired refinements. Learn sections of program with single jumps, then sections with double and triple jumps. Skate show program in shows and exhibitions.	Start full run-throughs of programs with jumps as they were choreographed. Ask specific judges to observe program and give feedback about any needed changes. Skate show program in shows and exhibitions.	Debut the competitive program at exhibitions. Judges' critique to elicit feedback about programs in this form. First competition for most skaters. Full run-throughs continue. Increase off-ice aerobic capacity. Mental training increases.	Further refine the competitive programs taking into account any changes from judges' critique. First major non-qualifying competition involving travel for most skaters. Full run-throughs continue. Increase off-ice aerobic capacity. Mental training increases.

• •

August	September	October	November	December	January
Skater should have good command of technical elements in program. Polish the artistic components in programs. More competitions, including summer invitationals. Full run-throughs continue. Increase off-ice aerobic capacity. Mental training increases.	Program training ramps up through last week of September. Competitions, including those involving travel. Maybe a few days off. Mental training—competition focusing. Full run-throughs continue. Increase off-ice aerobic capacity.	Strike balance between high degree of preparation and overtraining. Work in front of mirror to get performance points strong. Continue run-throughs but don't overtrain. Be rested and ready. Regional Competitions	Regional Competitions (At high level of preparation, but not quite at the peak.) Nonqualifying divisions reach peak.	Sectional Competition Intermediate-level skaters reach peak	National Competition Reach your peak.

NOTE: Regional, sectional, and national competition dates can vary from year to year. International competitions are held year round.

Getting Physically and Mentally Ready for Competitions and Tests

Competition Season Checklist

Activity	Date Must Be Completed	Check When Completed
Music cut and copies made		
Complete and mail application for major summer competition		
Complete and mail application for major fall competition		
Complete and mail application for regional competition		
Costume made for short program		
Costume made for long program		
Club simulation scheduled		
Feedback from judges requested		
Formal critique scheduled		
Skates sharpened		
Skates polished		
Hair cut or styled		
Visit to competition site		
Homework requested from teachers		
Photos completed		
Copies of photos made for programs		
Program photos mailed		
Relatives informed and invited to attend a particular event		

Packing List for Travel to a Competition or Exhibition

Have You Have Packed It?

- [ ] Skating bag—Carry-on luggage
- [ ] Costumes—Carry-on luggage
- [ ] Skates—Carry-on luggage
- [ ] Laces—Carry-on luggage
- [ ] Tights (bring extra)—Carry-on luggage
- [ ] Program music (bring extra copies)—Carry-on luggage
- [ ] Glasses and contacts (bring spares)—Carry-on luggage
- [ ] Medications (if applicable)—Carry-on luggage
- [ ] Extra costume
- [ ] Practice outfits
- [ ] Audio tape player and head phones
- [ ] Relaxation tapes
- [ ] Make-up
- [ ] Hair bows, clips
- [ ] Healthy snack foods
- [ ] Water bottle
- [ ] Tissues
- [ ] Sweater or sweatshirt for practice
- [ ] Camera and film
- [ ] Homework
- [ ] Books, magazines
- [ ] Toiletries
- [ ] First aid for feet kit (gel packs, moleskin, etc.)
- [ ] Sewing supplies and extra beads (if costume is beaded)

Imagination Exercise for Preparing for Competition Early in the Season

1.   Find a comfortable place to sit with your head supported. Let your muscles relax as much as possible as you settle into your seat. You might want to try the breathing exercise given on page 42–44 to help you feel calm.

2.   Gently close your eyes. If you visualize, let yourself create images that are sharp, clear, and vivid. If you do not think in images, imagine the feeling of preparing for competition, hearing the relevant sounds, and even smelling the scents that you associate with the places mentioned in this imagination exercise.

3.   Begin to imagine the rink in which you will be competing early in the season, perhaps a summer invitational in August. Imagine that you arrive there with time to spare. You check out the facility, find everything you need, and start your warm-up.

4.   Imagine that you feel like you are there with several months of training already completed and realizing that you still have enough time ahead to be truly ready for the first qualifying competition.

5.   Feel the sense of excitement about starting the season and being eager to skate your program for spectators and judges.

6.   Imagine yourself ready to use this experience to get feedback from people, information that will help you polish your program for later this fall.

7.   Imagine that you feel pleased at how you have trained your program so far and that you are excited about people seeing it. Stay with this feeling for a few moments.

8.   When you are ready, slowly open your eyes and notice that you are smiling and feeling glad about this early competition.

NOTE: A complete version of this imagination exercise and the one on page 107 is available on our audio tape set, *Skate Your Personal Best: Sound Advice.*

Skating Your Personal Best in Competitions and on Test Days

Imagination Exercise for Remaining Calm as You Begin Your Competition Practice Ice

1. Find a comfortable place to sit with your head supported. Let your muscles relax as much as possible as you settle into your seat. You might want to try the breathing exercise given on page 42–44 to help you feel calm.

2. Gently close your eyes. If you visualize, let yourself create images that are sharp, clear, and vivid. If you do not think in images, imagine the feeling of preparing for competition, hearing the relevant sounds, and even smelling the scents that you associate with the places mentioned in this imagineering exercise.

3. Imagine the rink(s) in which the first qualifying competition takes place. Imagine that you are walking in the door of the rink in which you will be skating your practice ice. Notice the building, the lights, the ice, the temperature. Feel yourself taking in all this information and feeling OK about being there.

4. Notice that you are wearing a comfortable practice outfit that you like. Notice that you are rested. Imagine that you look around at the other skaters already on the ice. If your mind starts to make any comparisons, tell yourself what *you* are here to do. Repeat your performance goal to yourself, perhaps, "I will skate my personal best as I compete here. Right now I am going to focus on my practicing and let everything else fade into the background."

5. Notice your competitors around you and that you feel confident, pleased to be there, and focused on your own skating.

6. Imagine that you can remain very focused on your own skating and programs during the entire time you are at the competition site. Feel this sense of confidence for a few moments. When you are ready, slowly open your eyes and notice that you are smiling.

℘ *Techniques Designed Specifically for Focusing and Refocusing at Competitions*

This is the very best time for you to be really caught up in your personal best goals and thinking about your skating—which is what *you* can control. Remember, this is not the best time to be preoccupied with your dream goals. Focusing on yourself and your performing helps keep you strong and calm.

Also keep in mind that "skating a clean short program" is an outcome goal. If you have decided you must skate clean and you then fall on an opening jump, your focus and confidence may disappear. This is because, with an outcome goal like "winning" or "skating clean," it is harder for you to recover quickly from an error and go on to finish strong. A performance goal is much more helpful for actual competition. You can keep going, recover if you need to, and skate to a wonderful finish.

Write your performance goal for your short program here.

An example might be: "I will skate my short program with good speed, enthusiam, and high energy. I will go for *everything.*" _____

_____

_____

_____

If you start to be distracted by competitors or anything else, you can use these refocusing internal-coaching statements. These focusing statements include those that put your attention on your body and those that put your attention on a particular personal best skating thought.

"I am prepared, ready, and excited."

"I feel my feet, my arms, and my hands."

"I am here, right now, ready to go."

"I can skate my best right here and now."

"I can skate like I love to skate—which I do!"

"I can get into my music and skate with inspiration."

"I am well trained and rested and ready to go."

Write your own focusing statement here. _____

_____

_____

_____

If you find yourself comparing your skating to someone else's, it can set off anxiety and impair your ability to focus and perform your best. What can you do if your thoughts have shifted to another skater and away from yourself?

1. Get your breathing under control. Use the "breathe in–pause–breathe out" pacing sequence to regulate your breath.
2. Although you did just get into a comparison that's upsetting you, remind yourself that you can refocus on you and get back in control again.
3. Ask yourself, "What do I have control over?"
4. Answer your question convincingly. "I have control over me and my skating. What other skaters do and what the judges decide is not possible for me to control. I can skate for myself and let the results take care of themselves."
5. Repeat your performance goal for your program to yourself.
6. Remind yourself that you know what to do exactly if you make a mistake. You will smile, keep going, and skate a strong finish.
7. Breathe again. Imagine yourself skating your short program as you have on your best practice days.
8. Remind yourself that you want to do this for yourself because you love it.

⤸ Techniques Designed Specifically for Generating an Optimal Mental Attitude Between the Short and Long Program

Whether you have placed first or last in the short, there is considerable room for your skating to go either way during the long program. The hours in between these two skates may become the most important time you can spend during a competition. During this gap is when Tracy and I really see how skaters' mental training skills can help them. When a skater has few skills for managing mental comparisons with competitors or calming nervousness or overcoming self-doubt, he or she can fall apart before the long program and consequently, skate it poorly even though well-trained.

Why is this time so crucial? In our experience, during this gap a skater is tempted to figure out what he or she needs to do for the long program—but based on what *others* did in the short. We find skaters talking about, "I can still be in the top four if I beat out_____." Or we hear, "Well, it doesn't matter how I skate now in the long. I can't raise my standing well enough to qualify for Sectionals."

This focus on other skaters and outcome goals is precisely what we caution against when young people prepare to skate in competition. Trying to figure out how to control what you can't is nerve-wracking and anxiety-provoking. We find skaters who skated well in the short because they focused on performance goals like "I will go out there and skate my best," can still get carried away by the temptation of thinking "Now I'm going to win!"

Tracy and I observe that a skater behaving arrogantly about her high placement in the short can be overtaken in the long program by a come-from-behind competitor. It is unwise to take for granted that you will be among the top four in the long program because you were first in the short. The short program accounts for only one third of the total score. Being complacent going into the long program can be a trap just as much as giving up because of a low placement.

What works best mentally between the short and the long programs?

You can perform better by staying involved in your own skating. Let others talk about comparisons while you keep a sharp focus on your performance goal for the long. If you are mentally zeroing in on getting into your music and attacking your long program, you will be less distracted. If you can walk away from discussions about final placements and go to practice ice with the intention of preparing to skate your best later in competition, you will be less nervous.

If one of your competitors is behaving badly and doing things to distract you and psych you out, you will be more likely to skate well in spite of this disruption if you are focused like a laser beam on only your own skating. Although many skaters like to socialize between the short and the long programs, we recommend that you almost stay in a bubble, remaining focused, well rested, and less stressed. The party at the end of the competition comes soon enough. We see skaters benefit when they stay out of the fray and more focused on themselves for this time period.

Write your own version of the following stategies which are good ways to keep yourself together between the short and long programs.

Imagine yourself staying calm and unruffled up to the time of the long program.
Write a little script here. _____

_____

_____

_____

Imagine yourself feeling ready and confident on the warm-up before your long.
Write a little script here. _____

_____

_____

_____

Imagine yourself in your start position, feeling ready and focused on skating your best.
Write a little script here. _____

_____

_____

_____

Write what you could say to yourself as you push off and begin your long program using words that will help you stay focused on performing your very best.

_____

_____

_____

_____

Write what you could say to yourself as you near the end of your long program to encourage yourself to skate a strong finish. _____

_____

_____

_____

What would you say to a competitor who gives you a hard time about staying off by yourself (like you are being "stuck up") before the long program?

_____

_____

_____

_____

ᑌ *Taking Care of Yourself for Personal Best Skating in Competition*

A particular challenge when skaters travel to competitions is finding healthy food to eat and getting enough rest. We offer some suggestions here for planning how you can eat well, snack well, and sleep well.

1. Bring healthy snacks with you. Some ideas for what you might pack in your suitcase are: protein bars, granola bars, protein powder, pretzels, trail mix, and dried fruit.

2. If your hotel room has a refrigerator, have your parents shop at a nearby grocery store for you. Ideas for snacks in your room are: lowfat yogurt, sliced chicken or turkey for sandwiches, string (mozarella) cheese, cottage cheese, fruit and fruit juice, lowfat milk, single serving cans of tuna, cereal, pita bread, and tofu.

3. At a restaurant, avoid fried foods that can slow you down physically and make you feel mentally sluggish. If your sweet tooth is active, try ordering sorbet, frozen yogurt, jello, or fruit for dessert. You might go to a juice bar and order fresh juice or a smoothie.

4. If you are going out to a restaurant before practice ice, be sure to allow enough time for your meal to be served, for you to properly digest it, and for you to arrive at the rink on time.

5. Keep to your regular mealtime schedule as much as possible.

6. You may be sharing a hotel room with several other people. Negotiate a reasonable bedtime that comes close to what yours is at home.

7. Get as many hours of sleep each night as you can. Quick twenty-minute naps during the afternoon may also help. If you find that napping is strange for you, lie down for twenty minutes to read or listen to quiet music.

8. If you are having difficulty getting to sleep at night, try a very hot bath and warm milk. The combination helps most people feel sleepy. Also, listen to the "Getting to Sleep" tape in our audiotape series, *Skate Your Personal Best: Sound Advice.*

✑ *Going Home After a Competition*

Here are some suggestions for planning your trip home and debriefing your experience of the competition after it is over.

1. Imagine the trip home.

Who will you want to talk to when you return home?_____

_____

_____

2. Imagine that you are *not* satisfied with your experience. Plan what you would say to someone important to you who asks you "did you win?"

Write what you would say here. _____

_____

_____

3. Imagine that you are satisfied with your experience. Plan what you would say to someone important to you who asks you "did you win?"

*Write what you would say here.*_____

_____

_____

4. ***What could you say to yourself to keep yourself encouraged about your skating if you are not happy with the outcome?*** _____

_____

5. ***What would you say to yourself if you were very pleased with your experience?***

_____

_____

ℭ *Evaluating Your Experience at a Competition*

Tracy and I find that reviewing a competition experience with a skater is a valuable activity. It helps a skater debrief and talk through any feelings he or she may have, and provides information about what can be refined and improved for even better competition experiences in the future. When we do this, we are looking for more than the skater's end result. The forms on these pages can be copied for use after each competition this year.

Name of Competition _____ **Date** _____

Location _____

Event(s) Skated _____

_____

What was your outcome goal for this competition, if you had one?

_____

Rate the extent to which you met this outcome goal.

Circle one or write in your own rating.

1. I did not meet my goal at all.   2. I somewhat met my goal.   3. I totally met my goal.

_____

Using the 10-point scale below:

1=No nervousness at all   to   10=the worst nervousness I have ever felt

Rate your level of nervousness during your first practice ice session _____

Rate your level of nervousness just before your short program _____

Rate your level of nervousness just before your long program _____

What mental strategies did you use for managing your nervousness?

_____

_____

_____

Describe how these strategies worked or didn't work for you. _____

_____

_____

_____

What mental preparation strategies did you use in the days **before** *the competition?*

_____

_____

_____

Describe how these strategies worked or didn't work for you. _____

_____

_____

_____

Describe your experience with your competitors. _____

_____

_____

_____

Is there anything you would do differently in responding to your competitors at the

next competition? If yes, what that would be? _____

_____

_____

_____

Think about the way you talked to yourself during this competition. What words made you nervous, if any? _____

_____

_____

Think about the way you talked to yourself during this competition. What words made you feel more confident, if any? _____

_____

_____

What did you really like about this competition that you would like to experience again?

_____

_____

_____

What did you really like about this competition that you would like to change?

_____

_____

_____

What could you do to make these changes before the next competition?

_____

_____

_____

⌒ *Strategies for Skating Your Personal Best on Test Days*

Most skaters don't get too concerned that they have an outcome goal for a test day, because that goal is usually "I want to pass."

Many skaters handle this outcome goal just fine. Others can become upset about the test day and worry about what the judges will do. They may also worry about feeling embarrassed if they don't pass.

If a skater is unusually nervous about a test day, it may mean that he or she is just not ready. Talking with the coach about postponing the date may be wise so the skater can further train for the specific moves, elements, or dance that will be tested.

Tracy and I have observed that it helps even when you just want to pass a test to have a performance goal for skating well on a test day. A performance goal can be "I am prepared and will skate these moves/elements/dances as well as I can, like I have on my best practice." A performance goal such as this will help you stay focused.

Write a performance goal that would be appropriate for your next test day.

_____

_____

_____

_____

As in competitions, quite a few skaters are distressed by the idea that there are judges at the rail who are evaluating and observing the skaters' performance. Tracy and I have found a little trick that might help with this, so you can be more focused and feel more calm. First, be certain that you are prepared and have as your goal defined performance criteria. Then allow yourself to imagine that the judges are unknown to you. Imagine that as you come on to the ice to skate your test, you can hear and follow the judges' instructions, but you don't really notice who they are. They seem nameless and faceless to you.

This suggestion has helped several prepared—but nervous—skaters that we know feel much less nervous, by depersonalizing the judging process for a test day.

Pair Skating

As a former pair skater herself, Tracy has some great experience for skaters thinking about skating pairs. She recommends that you ask yourself these questions before pursuing this exciting and challenging kind of skating.

Do I currently skate singles?   ☐ *Yes*   ☐ *No*

If I do skate singles and want to skate pairs, how will I find sufficient time to train in both? _____

_____

_____

If I do skate singles and want to skate pairs, how will I find sufficient financial resources to skate both? _____

_____

_____

What is my current level in singles? _____

What elements do I need to pass in my next level of testing in order to present myself as a prospective partner who is motivated to learn? _____

_____

_____

What am I looking for in a partner? _____

_____

Am I willing to move in order to be near a partner? ☐ *Yes* ☐ *No*

If I cannot move, how will I assist a new partner in moving to be near me so we can train together? (What financial resources can my family provide? What assistance with housing and a job can my family offer a partner?) _____

_____

_____

_____

What contacts do I have for finding a partner? _____

_____

_____

What tryouts can I attend? _____

_____

_____

_____

What do I have prepared to send to a prospective partner or a pair coach?
(Videotape of my singles highlights; videotape of me skating with a former partner; a résumé of my experience; cover letters; letters of recommendation from coaches.)

_____

_____

_____

_____

If you are currently skating pairs, answering these questions may be helpful in becoming more aware of things that will strengthen your relationship.

Who takes the lead in decisions that my coach gives to us?

☐ *I do*   ☐ *My partner does*

How do we resolve disagreements with each other? _____

_____

_____

_____

What can we do to improve our communication skills as people who are skating together? _____

_____

_____

_____

What are our pair goals for this coming year? _____

_____

_____

_____

Who can help us when we get into a problem that we can't seem to solve ourselves?

_____

_____

_____

_____

When a pair is in conflict, it can be terribly stressful. Tracy and I want to share two ideas from a book on negotiation called *Getting to Yes,* by Roger Fisher and William Ury. They suggest that when two sides in a conflict have been fighting or are just stuck in disagreement, that they "go to the balcony." By this statement, the authors mean that the two sides take a time out, or a little break. During this break, each side cools off and rests. Each side then thinks about what is important to them as a team.

This break helps them be ready for the second suggestion, that they "keep their eyes on the prize." This means to remember why you two got together in the first place. It means to think about the early days together, when there was the excitement of starting out with a joint goal in mind.

These two ideas can be used with good results by members of a pair team who are upset with each other or not getting along. First, think about how you would "go to the balcony" during a lesson or practice in a way that would not be too disruptive or take too much of your coach's time, but still let you calm down and cool off.

Write your ideas here. _____

_____

Now think about what your joint goals are. If you both have "your eyes on the prize," what are you going after—together? What is it that you are pursuing as a team that you have devoted so much time to already?

Write your ideas here. _____

_____

_____

_____

Write your original reason for getting together as a team.—_____

_____

_____

For Skaters and Parents Together

Tracy and I recognize the importance for skaters of having the support of their parents as they pursue their skating goals. We work closely with parents to make certain that parents know what the skater needs in terms of time for lessons and practice, transportation, and financial resources to pay for ice time, lessons, costumes, music, choreography, travel, competition entry fees, skates, ballet classes, and off-ice conditioning.

In the following questions, discuss with your parents how things are working for you as a team.

Working together, you can make skating a rewarding part of life.

What is working for you as a team of skater and parents? _____

_____

_____

_____

What do you need to improve? _____

_____

_____

_____

What outside resources do you have to assist you? _____

_____

_____

_____

Adult Skaters and Their Unique Needs

Adult skaters are involved in a wonderful sport at a point in their lives when many of those around them on the ice are younger. Tracy and I suggest that you think about your goals in skating again on these pages, in addition to the goal-setting process earlier in this workbook.

How many hours per week do you have for training? ———————————————

What financial resources can you devote each month to training? ————————

What are your desires in skating as an adult? (Do you want to skate for the exercise? Do you want to see how much you can learn? Do you want to compete? If you competed when you were younger and did well, do you want to compete as a Senior [if you are 25 to 29] or do you want to compete in adult competitions?)

———————————————————————————————————————

———————————————————————————————————————

If you have not skated before and have not competed in skating or another sport before, whose guidance about competition worries can you seek?

———————————————————————————————————————

How much time can you spend doing off-ice conditioning? (This conditioning for flexibility, strength, balance, and coordination is very important for adults in order to skate comfortably and prevent injury.) ————————————————————

Where can you find a suitable instructor to guide you in your off-ice training?

Where can you get personalized advice about your nutritional needs for skating in a healthy manner? ————————————————————————————————